BOUSILLE
AND THE JUST

Inquiries about the production of this play
in English should be addressed to the publisher,
Irwin Publishing Inc.,
180 West Beaver Creek Road,
Richmond Hill, Ontario L4B 1B4

BOUSILLE
and the Just

GRATIEN GÉLINAS

Translated from the French by
KENNETH JOHNSTONE
and
JOFFRE MIVILLE-DECHÊNE

IRWIN PUBLISHING

Toronto, Canada

Copyright, Canada, 1961
by Gratien Gélinas

First published in paperback format 1966

ISBN 0 7720 0193 6

4 5 6 7 8 9 10 11 12   JD   92 91 90 89 88 87 86 85 84

Printed in Canada

CHARACTERS

The first performance in English of *Bousille and the Just* was given on the stage of La Comédie Canadienne in Montreal on February 23, 1961, with the following cast:

BELLBOY	Yves Gélinas
PHIL VÉZINA	Paul Berval
HENRI GRAVEL	Yves Létourneau
AURORE VÉZINA	Béatrice Picard
BOUSILLE	Gratien Gélinas
MOTHER	Juliette Huot
NOELLA GRAVEL	Hélène Loiselle
LAWYER	Paul Hébert
BROTHER THÉOPHILE	Gilles Latulippe
COLETTE RICHARD	Ginette Letondal

TIME

The present.

ACT I, Scene 1: Morning of the first day, around eight-thirty.

        Scene 2: Evening of the first day, around six.

ACT II, Scene 1: Morning of the second day, around nine.

        Scene 2: Afternoon of the second day, around four-thirty.

BOUSILLE
AND THE JUST

ACT ONE

SCENE ONE

THE SCENE *is set in the cheap room of a second-rate hotel near the Court House in Montreal. A small entry leading to the door facing the audience, a closet on the left, and the bathroom on the right, divides the back wall into almost equal parts. Two dressers of different heights, one with a mirror, stand against the back wall on each side of this entry. Against the left wall is a small desk with a telephone; upstage, a door leads to an adjoining room, probably furnished in the same drab style. Against the right wall, foreground, in front of the window, are an armchair and the inevitable radiator, and farther upstage stand the bed and a small night-table.*

Rough usage has left its mark on the furniture and bed clothes, which obviously were never of high quality. The walls, adorned with trite and meaningless pictures, have that tired tint which reflects years of dust and smoke.

When the curtain rises, the room is empty. Then a key turns in the lock. The door opens and a BELLBOY *comes in, carrying a small suitcase and a bag, which he sets down on the luggage rack at the foot of the bed. During the ensuing dialogue, he raises the blind and opens the door to the adjoining room.*

PHIL, *carrying a wrapped bottle, has come in behind him, and stops to survey the room.*

PHIL: Just what we need—eh, Henri?

HENRI, *following him in:*   Out of my way! I've got to call the lawyer. There's no time to lose. [*He rushes to the*

3

telephone, and consults a slip of paper he has taken out of his pocket.]

PHIL, *throwing the bottle on the bed*: No time to lose for me, either. [*He makes a beeline for the bathroom.*]

HENRI, *holding the receiver and handing a tip to the* BELL- BOY: Here.

BELLBOY: Thank you, sir. [*He goes out.*]

HENRI, *on the telephone*: Regent 3-4516. . . . One six. . . . Right.

AURORE, *who has just come in*: Where's Phil?

HENRI, *nodding towards the bathroom*: In there.

AURORE, *taking off her coat and throwing it on the bed*: Don't forget to call the lawyer.

HENRI: What do you think I'm doing now?

AURORE: He's not the only one in Montreal you could be calling! [*She is visibly under a nervous strain.*] All right, let's all start squabbling this morning! That should fix things!

HENRI, *on the telephone*: Well, never mind. . . . Thanks. [*He hangs up, disturbed.*]

AURORE: No answer?

HENRI: No.

AURORE: What's the matter with him? Loafing in bed, when he's due in court in three quarters of an hour!

HENRI, *consulting his watch*: Twenty to nine; maybe he's still at home. I'll call him there. [*He looks for a number on his slip of paper.*]

AURORE, *glancing into the adjoining room*: You took two rooms?

HENRI, *on the telephone*: Get me Victor 4-5843.

AURORE: This trial is going to cost us plenty!

HENRI: So what? There are six of us: two beds are hardly too many.

AURORE *shrugs and disappears into the next room.*

HENRI, *nervous on the telephone*: Hello! Mrs. Fontaine?
. . . Can I have a word with your husband? . . . Oh!
How long ago? . . . Henri Gravel, from St. Tite. . . . How
do you do? . . . Yes, he's supposed to defend my brother
Bruno in court at ten o'clock. . . . That's right. . . . Do
you think he was going straight to his office? . . . I see.
. . . Well, I'll call him there in fifteen minutes. . . . Look,
I wouldn't want to miss him for anything; so if you
hear from him before I do will you have him call me
right away at the Corona Hotel, Room . . . [*Asking an
empty room.*] What's our room number? [*Finds it on
the telephone dial.*] Room 312. . . . [*Volubly.*] Excuse
me for bothering you like this, but you can understand,
we're all in a sweat today. We'd planned to be here at
eight sharp, but we had a flat, just coming out of Louise-
ville. . . . Fine. . . . You've made a note of it? Room 312,
Corona Hotel. . . . It's just a block from the Court
House. . . . Thank you, Mrs. Fontaine, that's very good
of you. . . . [*He starts to hang up, but changes his mind.*]
Oh, by the way, do you happen to know what room the
trial is being held in? . . . Hello! [*He hangs up.*]

PHIL, *coming out of the bathroom, relieved*: There!
That's better!

HENRI: I've just talked to his wife.

PHIL, *at a loss*: Whose wife?

HENRI: The lawyer's, idiot!

PHIL: Okay, okay! Simmer down, my dear brother-in-
law! Why so jumpy?

HENRI: It's easy to see that you're not the one who's been
rotting behind bars these last four months!

PHIL: Believe me, I'm just as upset as you are.

HENRI: No kidding!

AURORE *returns from the next room.*

PHIL: Ask your sister. She'll tell you how I've been tossing
around in bed for a week!

AURORE: Snoring your head off! [*To* HENRI.] So what story did the lawyer's wife give you?

HENRI: She said he should be at his office in fifteen minutes at the most.

AURORE: If I were you, I'd go and wait for him there.

HENRI: Maybe I will. It's just around the corner.

AURORE: Go ahead! I'll feel a lot better when you get hold of him.

Enter BOUSILLE, *breathless, carrying a thermos bottle and, under his arm, the morning papers.*

PHIL: Here's Bousille—with the papers.

HENRI, *snatching the papers away from* BOUSILLE: Come on, hurry up! [*Throwing one on the bed and opening the other.*] I told you to make it snappy.

BOUSILLE: I'm sorry, Henri: I had to run two blocks.

AURORE: Where did you leave Mamma?

BOUSILLE: In the lobby with Henri's wife. She's resting a while. Did you reach the lawyer?

AURORE, *over* PHIL's *shoulder, while he looks through the second paper*: St. Anthony, I promise you a high mass if we don't find anything about it in here.

BOUSILLE, *to* PHIL: I parked the car in the lot across the street. Here are the keys. [*He drops them into* PHIL's *coat pocket, as the latter, absorbed in his paper, does not answer.*] Excuse me for a moment. [*To* AURORE.] I'm going down to help Noella bring your mother up. [*From the door.*] In case you've forgotten, we really should call the lawyer. [*Exit.*]

AURORE, *pacing back and forth, grumbling*: First of all, Gisèle catches whooping cough in the spring, then Mamma gets high blood pressure in the summer, then *he* lands in court in the fall! What's going to happen in the winter?

PHIL, *finding something in the paper*: Well, stop worrying, Kitten: you won't have to pay for that high mass, after all!

AURORE: Oh, no! Don't tell me! [*She comes closer, as does* HENRI.]

PHIL: We're lucky; it's just a paragraph, tucked away in a corner.

HENRI: Go on, read it!

PHIL, *reading*: "Bruno Gravel On Trial. This morning at ten o'clock in the Court of Queen's Bench, Bruno Gravel of St. Tite will appear before Mr. Justice Bernard Martin. Gravel, a bachelor of 24, is accused of murder in connection wtih the death of Marc Lepage, 22, of Montreal. The fatality resulted from a brawl on May 30th last in a St. Lambert restaurant."

AURORE, *in despair*: Dear God! We're really going to drain the cup—right down to the bitter dregs!

PHIL: What difference does it make? Everybody we know has heard about it.

AURORE: A respectable family like ours! [*Snapping her fingers.*] Never had *that much* trouble with the law.

PHIL: Sure, we're respectable people. That's why the Good Lord won't leave us in this bloody mess.

HENRI, *between his teeth*: All that matters is to get him out of this with his nose clean!

PHIL: That'll be easy: he's innocent.

AURORE: Of course he is. There's no doubt about it!

PHIL: Just wait till the judge announces "Not guilty" from the Bench: that'll shut them up in St. Tite.

HENRI, *obsessed with one idea*: I'll get him out of this with his nose clean or my name's not Henri Gravel.

PHIL: You're so damn stubborn, you'll swing it all right.

HENRI, *as the door opens*: Careful! Here comes Mamma.

AURORE, *to* PHIL: Hide the newspapers!

They try to conceal them as the MOTHER *enters, sup-*

7

ported by NOELLA. BOUSILLE *follows, carrying a bag and a small radio.*

MOTHER: There's something in the papers!

AURORE: No, no! Now stop fretting over nothing! [*She raises her voice when speaking to the* MOTHER, *who wears a small hearing aid.*]

PHIL: I was just looking through the sports pages.

NOELLA: Let me take your coat, Mrs. Gravel.

MOTHER: No, I'll keep it on; you know what I said, Noella.

BOUSILLE, *aside, to the others*: She's set on seeing Bruno right away: she didn't even want to come up.

AURORE: Seeing Bruno! What for?

MOTHER: To comfort him, of course!

HENRI: This morning is hardly the time.

MOTHER: If he doesn't need his mother today, poor darling, when will he need her?

HENRI, *drily to the* MOTHER: Listen: don't you start making a nuisance of yourself. We've got enough on our hands already. [*To* AURORE.] I'm off to the lawyer's.

AURORE, *as he goes out*: Try not to miss him.

MOTHER: This is a silly idea you all have, keeping me from seeing him!

NOELLA, *insisting gently*: Take off you coat; you'll be too warm.

MOTHER, *giving in reluctantly*: At times, Noella, your husband is very hard on his poor mother.

AURORE: Can't you understand? The lawyer told Henri last week: during the trial the accused is not allowed visitors.

MOTHER: "The accused, the accused!" Must you use that word? You know very well he's innocent.

AURORE: *We* know it. But the judge doesn't, yet. That's why there must be a trial.

8

MOTHER: Locked up in a cell like a criminal ever since last May! And he wouldn't even hurt a fly!

PHIL: Never mind, Mother. The trial will clear everything up. Then you can go on babying him to your heart's content.

MOTHER: At least you'll let me go to the Court House?

AURORE, *firmly*: This morning you're going to stay right here and be quiet. With your blood pressure you have to take care not to get too upset.

MOTHER: But . . . this afternoon?

AURORE: This afternoon, maybe, if you promise to behave.

MOTHER: I promise.

AURORE: And not start bawling in front of everybody.

MOTHER, *turning to* BOUSILLE: Bousille, in the meantime, get me his picture from my bag.

BOUSILLE: Right away, Auntie.

PHIL, *aside to* AURORE: You know, it might be a good idea.

AURORE: What?

PHIL: For her to show up over there. Nothing softens up a jury like seeing the mother of the accused burst into tears in court.

AURORE: Well, I hope we won't have to depend on that.

BOUSILLE, *handing the* MOTHER *a small framed picture of* BRUNO *at his first communion*: Here, Auntie.

MOTHER: Put it on the dresser with that statue of Blessed St. Ann that I brought along.

BOUSILLE: Very well, Auntie.

PHIL, *looking at the photograph*: You might have picked a more recent picture. You'd never guess from this that he's a big, husky guy, six foot tall.

MOTHER: He has grown up, but he hasn't changed.

NOELLA, *who has been busying herself quietly between the*

9

rooms: Why don't you lie down on the bed? You'll be more comfortable.

MOTHER: I'd rather sit up. I can't breathe, lying down with my corset on.

AURORE: Do you still feel that knot in your stomach?

MOTHER: I think it's getting tighter.

AURORE: Have a good cry; it will help. Now is the time to let your hair down: we're only the family.

MOTHER: I know it would do me good, but I just can't.

PHIL, *pouring himself a drink from his bottle*: Don't hold back, dear lady, don't hold back. Let the steam out!

MOTHER: Bousille, give me my bag. I want my beads.

BOUSILLE: Right away, Auntie. [*Coming back with the handbag.*] I just plugged in your little radio: it'll be ready for the Family Rosary broadcast at seven o'clock.

MOTHER: I mustn't forget.

BOUSILLE: Depend on me to remind you.

MOTHER, *searching her handbag*: Good heavens! Aurore!

AURORE: What's the matter?

MOTHER: I've lost my beads!

AURORE, *approaching*: You're sure they're not in your bag? [*She looks herself.*]

MOTHER: My lovely rosary of the Third Order!

NOELLA: Did you use it in the car?

MOTHER: No. Today of all days, when I need it so badly to pray for Bruno!

AURORE: I'll bet anything, in all your excitement you left it at home.

MOTHER: Then 'phone right away. I must know.

AURORE: Sure, we'll spend two bucks on a 'phone call for a rosary worth seventy-five cents!

NOELLA: If it will set her mind at rest, why not?

PHIL: Go ahead and call: I should speak to Roland at the garage, anyway.

AURORE: No wonder we're always broke! [*She goes to the telephone.*]

MOTHER: Blessed St. Ann, I promise to burn three big dollar candles if I find it.

PHIL: Hold on a minute, before you promise: maybe it's no more lost than you are.

AURORE, *on the telephone*: Hello, Operator. Will you get me St. Tite, 3684? . . . Anyone there. . . .

BOUSILLE, *offering his beads*: Auntie, I can lend you mine, if you wish.

MOTHER: No, I want my own beads!

PHIL: You're right: once you get the feel of a good tool, it's always hard to change.

AURORE, *on the telephone*: Hello, Gaston? Mummy speaking, dear. Listen: go into Granny's bedroom and see if you can find her beads anywhere.

MOTHER: Tell him to look under my pillow.

AURORE, *on the telephone*: Look under her pillow first. Make it fast. In the meantime, let me speak to Gisèle.

PHIL: Don't forget, I want to talk to Roland.

AURORE, *on the telephone*: Hello, Gisèle. . . . If Mrs. Larose doesn't arrive before you go to school, leave the key with her on your way. If she asks you anything about Uncle Bruno, tell her you don't know a thing. . . . If you're a good girl Mummy will bring you a nice present. . . . No, not something useful.

PHIL, *under his breath*: A lovely prayer-book!

AURORE, *on the telephone*: What? . . . [*To the* MOTHER.] Your beads were there, of course.

MOTHER, *relieved*: Thank you, good St. Ann!

AURORE, *on the telephone*: No, the trial is far from over. It hasn't even started yet. . . . I don't know. . . . Maybe we'll be home tonight. . . . It all depends.

11

MOTHER: I want to sleep in my own bed and get my beads.

AURORE, *on the telephone*:   Yes, yes. . . .

PHIL: Hey, take it easy: it's quite a jaunt, there and back.

AURORE, *on the telephone*:   Ring the garage downstairs: Daddy wants to speak to Roland. [*To* PHIL.] Come on, you!

PHIL, *going to the telephone*:   Besides, I have business in town tonight.

MOTHER, *stubbornly*:   I warn you, I won't spend the night in a hotel room without my beads, like . . . a . . . a floozie!

PHIL, *on the telephone*:   Hello!

BOUSILLE: Don't worry, Auntie, I'll drive you.

AURORE: Where?

BOUSILLE: To St. Tite. It would suit me fine; I'd like to go and look after the dog. The house is almost empty: he must feel pretty lonely.

PHIL, *on the telephone*:   Hello! Roland? . . . Phil speaking. . . . Say, that fellow who had the accident yesterday, has he come in yet for the estimate? . . . Take him for all he's worth, eh? He's from Toronto: we'll never see the sucker again, anyway. . . . Sure. . . . So long! [*He hangs up.*]

MOTHER, *sighing*:   I'll never get through the day without my beads!

PHIL, *picking up his glass again*:   I know. I'd feel the same way in your shoes.

BOUSILLE: Do you know what, Auntie? I've got a good mind to ask my little brother to come and keep you company.

MOTHER: What brother?

BOUSILLE: You remember, Edgar—Brother Théophile, as he's called in the Order.

MOTHER: How old is he?

BOUSILLE: Seventeen. He's my father's last child by his second marriage.

MOTHER, *vaguely remembering*: Oh, yes!

BOUSILLE: He's in the Noviciate on St. Hubert Street, not far from here.

PHIL, *to the Mother*: He'd sure trade in your old worry for a new model in a flash!

BOUSILLE, *candidly*: Of course.

MOTHER: Well, if you think he can comfort me. . . .

BOUSILLE: He's so pure, that boy! He was only eleven and a half when he entered the Order.

PHIL: Yeah! That sure gives him a broad experience of life.

BOUSILLE: I can go and bring him right away. Only last week he wrote me that today was a holiday in honour of the Brother Director.

PHIL: Okay! Go get him.

MOTHER, *as* BOUSILLE *prepares to leave*: You know, Aurore, I think I'll make myself comfortable on the bed in the other room.

AURORE: Of course. You should have done it before. [*They both disappear into the next room.*]

BOUSILLE, *to* PHIL: If the lawyer shows up, tell him I'll be back in five minutes.

PHIL: Fine! [*Affecting seriousness.*] As for your kid brother, don't forget to hold his hand when you cross the street!

BOUSILLE, *at a loss*: I beg your pardon?

HENRI *comes in with the* LAWYER.

HENRI: Mr. Fontaine, I want you to meet my wife.

LAWYER: How do you do, Mrs. Gravel?

HENRI, *presenting* PHIL: My brother-in-law, Phil Vézina.

13

PHIL, *shaking hands with the* LAWYER: Believe me, we've been expecting you like the doctor at a delivery.

AURORE, *enters from the next room and cuts off* BOUSILLE, *who was waiting, hand outstretched.*

PHIL, *introducing her*: Aurore, my chief of police.

AURORE: How do you do? You shouldn't have bothered to come here. We could have gone to your office.

LAWYER: It was simpler this way.

HENRI, *to* AURORE: Where's Mother?

AURORE: In the other room. She'll be along.

PHIL, *as* BOUSILLE *tugs his sleeve*: We nearly forgot one of your reluctant witnesses. [*Introducing him.*] Blaise Belzile. Better known in the world of organized vice as Bousille.

LAWYER: How do you do?

PHIL, *explaining*: A sort of distant cousin, 'way out in left field, on my wife's side.

LAWYER: Belzile? You are the only one here, I believe, who received a subpoena.

PHIL, *answering for* BOUSILLE, *who is speechless*: Quite right, yes.

AURORE: You've no idea how anxious he was to see you.

PHIL: He wants to go over his part with you before the show begins.

LAWYER, *to* BOUSILLE: Don't worry; we'll take time to get to the bottom of this thing. But not this morning. Anyway, it's very unlikely that you will be asked to testify today.

PHIL, *to* BOUSILLE: Waiting till tomorrow doesn't disappoint you too much?

BOUSILLE: Oh, as far as I'm concerned . . . there's no hurry—as long as—

LAWYER: If by chance things go more quickly I'll see you

between twelve and two. But I think it's safe enough to make an appointment at the end of the day.

AURORE, *as the* MOTHER *enters from the next room*: Mother, I want you to meet Mr. Fontaine, our lawyer. [*To the* LAWYER, *indicating the hearing aid*.] Please speak up.

LAWYER: How do you do, Mrs. Gravel?

MOTHER, *throwing herself on the* LAWYER: You'll save my Bruno for me, won't you?

LAWYER: Rest assured that I will do my best.

BOUSILLE, *aside to* PHIL: I'll go and get Théophile. [*Exit.*]

MOTHER, *taking the photograph from the dresser*: There's my poor little boy!

LAWYER, *kindly*: Why yes! I recognize him.

PHIL: You do? Well, I must say you're pretty good!

HENRI: Listen, Mamma: the trial starts in fifteen minutes and Mr. Fontaine has some questions to ask.

MOTHER: To ask me?

AURORE, *annoyed*: No, not you!

HENRI: So why don't you go back to the other room and stretch out for five minutes?

NOELLA: Come along, Mrs. Gravel, it's time for your injection.

MOTHER, *to the* LAWYER: Do your best, won't you? Like you never did before!

LAWYER: You can count on me.

MOTHER: Even though I haven't got my beads with me I'll try to pray for you. [*She disappears into the next room with* NOELLA]

LAWYER: Now, in the few minutes left to us, I'll try to sum up the case, as I see it, based on the evidence given at the coroner's inquest—[*To* HENRI.] and on the conversations we've had together.

AURORE: Listen, Mr. Fontaine, if you're in a hurry, I'll tell you in two words the why and wherefore of this whole mess. Bruno is just a poor helpless boy who had the bad luck to fall into the clutches of a little tramp, Colette Richard. A little tramp, who got him to fall head over heels in love with her and then made him completely miserable by purring at every tomcat who rubbed against her skirt. Finally he couldn't stand it any more, the poor kid. He got into a scrap with one of them and —God or the Devil willing, take your pick—it was the other one who fell and stayed there. That's the whole story.

HENRI: If he cracked his skull that's tough luck for him, but *I* say so much the worse for the guy who started the whole business.

LAWYER: *consulting his notes*: The accident occurred on the thirtieth of May, I believe?

AURORE: Yes, the very day that Noella and Henri were married.

LAWYER: Around four in the afternoon?

AURORE: We had just left for St. Tite.

HENRI: I didn't hear about it until after midnight, when Phil called me in Old Orchard.

PHIL: It broke my heart to spoil his honeymoon that way, but I had to.

LAWYER: The wedding took place in St. Lambert?

AURORE: Yes, in Noella's parish.

LAWYER: And the accident happened in a local restaurant?

AURORE: Yes—where Bruno caught them red-handed.

LAWYER: You mean Miss Richard and the deceased?

AURORE: Marc Lepage, yes.

LAWYER: Had they both attended the wedding?

AURORE: Yes. Imagine: Colette was the bridesmaid and Bruno the best man! As for that other one, he sneaked

16

into the wedding like a fox into a henhouse.

NOELLA, *coming from the other room to get something from the dresser*: Aurore, I beg your pardon: Marc did *not* sneak in. He was invited, like the other guests. After all, his brother has been married to my sister for five years.

HENRI *glares at her as she returns to the next room.*

AURORE: Ever since she became pregnant, she's been so touchy, that one!

PHIL, *to the* LAWYER: Don't mind her: we're all a bit on edge today.

LAWYER: I understand. Getting back to Miss Richard, I would like to know her attitude.

AURORE: Her attitude, her attitude! How can we tell? She hasn't set foot in St. Tite since that day. Except once, apparently, in the middle of the night, to pick up her things.

PHIL: I guess she was afraid of gossip.

HENRI: If you want to question her, my wife has her Montreal 'phone number.

LAWYER: That would be very helpful. I could see her at the same time as Mr. Delzile—if she agrees, of course.

HENRI: Don't worry: she'll come. [*He disappears into the other room.*]

PHIL: The worst of it is that none of the family was there when the brawl started.

AURORE: Just our luck. No witnesses, except that little bitch Colette—and Bousille, a lame brain with hardly enough sense to tell his right foot from his left!

PHIL: Don't run him down: he's pretty useful as an errand boy!

NOELLA: *entering from the next room*: Listen, Mr. Fontaine: Colette Richard was my best friend and she still

17

is. I won't do anything to get her mixed up in some dirty deal.

The others protest vaguely.

LAWYER: There is no question of a dirty deal about this, Mrs. Gravel. A lawyer has the right—and even the duty—to question consenting witnesses before the hearing.

HENRI, *grimly, to* NOELLA: There's no point in discussing it, just call her.

MOTHER: *who has followed* NOELLA *into the room, imploring her*: Do this for me, Noella dear. You'll know what it means to be a mother when your baby is born.

NOELLA: I'll 'phone her this afternoon.

HENRI: Call her right now; so we'll be sure.

LAWYER: Would you be good enough to make an appointment for six-thirty, here or at my office?

NOELLA, *on the telephone, while the conversation goes on*: Clairval 4-5376. . . .

AURORE, *to the* LAWYER: You might find it quieter here.

LAWYER: There would certainly be fewer interruptions.

PHIL: Yes sir! There's no place like a hotel room to have peace.

NOELLA, *on the telephone*: Hello! Miss Colette Richard, please. . . . Why, of course! I didn't recognize your voice: have you got a cold? . . . I understand, poor thing! . . . Yes, about half an hour ago. . . . Listen, Colette: I have something to ask you, but I don't want you to feel bound to—[*Talking, she carries the telephone into the next room, closing the door behind her.*]

AURORE, *who was listening with ears cocked, spitefully*: There are times when I wonder whether she's with us or against us!

HENRI, *curtly*: Never mind.

PHIL, *to the* LAWYER: Just between us, what are Bruno's

chances in the trial? We hardly know what to think: sometimes we fear the worst; sometimes we're sure he'll be released with apologies. What's your opinion? The judge can't hear you now.

LAWYER: You already know that, in view of the circumstances of the case and the evidence given by the police, he's facing a murder charge.

PHIL: You don't mean he could get ... the rope?

MOTHER, *with a sob*: No, it can't be!

AURORE, *close to tears also*: Please, Mother! Let's keep the little bit of sanity we have left.

LAWYER: I can assure you, Mrs. Gravel, that your son is in no such danger.

HENRI: He has a chance for acquittal? That's what we want to know.

LAWYER: Yes, a very good chance. I don't think the prosecution can prove the charge in its present form. Not only did the accused, to all appearances, have no intention of killing—

AURORE: Well, that's clear enough!

HENRI, *cutting her off again*: You listen!

LAWYER, *continuing*: —but also nothing so far proves that his assault was premeditated. Furthermore, I noted a very interesting detail in the coroner's report: it seems that what might be interpreted as the first blow was struck by the victim himself.

PHIL: You don't say!

LAWYER: If this is, more or less, an obvious case of legitimate self-defence, following physical and moral provocation on the part of the deceased, we are far from the implication of murder.

HENRI: Which means?

LAWYER: According to the spirit of the law, any doubt must favour the accused.

PHIL: And in your opinion, there is such a doubt?

19

LAWYER: So much so that tomorrow, after the examination of the Crown witnesses, I intend to ask that the case be dismissed and the accused released.

AURORE: God in heaven! If it were only possible!

LAWYER: Of course, I can't promise anything.

AURORE: If he's acquitted, won't we hold our heads up again?

PHIL: Oh, as far as I'm concerned, I never bowed mine.

MOTHER, *to the* LAWYER: Couldn't you ask the judge to do me a real big favour and release him right away?

LAWYER: I'm sorry, Mrs. Gravel, that's impossible.

MOTHER: Another eternity to wait! Dear St. Ann, will this never end?

NOELLA *returns from the other room with the telephone.*

HENRI: Well?

NOELLA: Colette will be here at six-thirty, provided I **go** and get her.

LAWYER: Thank you.

NOELLA: Not at all. [*She returns to the other room.*]

HENRI, *to the* LAWYER, *after consulting his watch*: I don't want to throw you out, but it's nearly twenty to ten.

LAWYER: Already? Then I must be going. I'll see you in court.

HENRI, *to the* LAWYER: You have all your papers?

LAWYER: Right here, yes. [*He replaces the file in his briefcase.*]

PHIL, *to the* LAWYER, *before pouring himself a last drink*: Mr. Fontaine, how about a few drops of liquid courage before the battle?

LAWYER, *smiling*: No, thank you.

PHIL, *helping himself*: Well, I'm taking no chances!

HENRI: What room is the trial in?

LAWYER, *searching his coat pocket*: I've made a note of it somewhere.

HENRI: You know, we've never been in the joint before, so maybe we'd better follow you.

LAWYER: As you wish.

BOUSILLE *has just come in with* BROTHER THÉOPHILE.

PHIL, *seeing the young lay brother, who smiles shyly, hat in hand*: Why, here comes our papal delegate!

BOUSILLE: Edgar, I think you know everyone here, except Mr. Fontaine, our lawyer. [*Introducing him proudly.*] The Reverend Brother Théophile, my young half-brother.

MOTHER, *taking* THÉOPHILE'S *arm*: Even if he's only a distant cousin, couldn't you take him along and show him to the judge, to prove we are respectable people?

LAWYER, *smiling*: Thank you, but I think we have better arguments to convince him of that. [*Taking his leave.*] So until tonight, Mrs. Gravel. And don't worry too much. [*Exit, followed by* HENRI.]

AURORE, *to* PHIL, *who is trying to empty his glass*: Come on, you slowpoke! [*The couple disappear through the door.*]

BOUSILLE: Wait for me. [*To* THÉOPHILE.] I have to rush out, too. . . . So I'll leave Auntie in your care: try to comfort her.

THÉOPHILE: I'll do my very best.

BOUSILLE *rushes out.*

NOELLA, *to* THÉOPHILE: May I take your hat? [*She takes it.*]

THÉOPHILE, *shyly*:   You're too kind.

MOTHER: My poor Théophile, it's so good of you to come and help me bear my cross.

THÉOPHILE, *sincerely*:   It is a pleasure for me, Auntie.

MOTHER: My! In the midst of life's miseries just the sight of a soutane cheers you up! Isn't that true, Noella?

NOELLA, *approaching the* MOTHER: You should lie down: it would do you good.

MOTHER, *submitting to* NOELLA: I worry just as much in one position as in another.

THÉOPHILE: Auntie, I've brought you a little gift, to cheer you up.

MOTHER: You did? [*Stretching out a weak hand.*] Let me see it.

THÉOPHILE, *taking it out of his pocket*: It's a medal of St. Jude, patron saint of hopeless causes.

MOTHER, *dropping her hand, moaning*: Put it on the dresser.

NOELLA *comes out of the bathroom and puts a damp towel over the* MOTHER'S *brow.*

MOTHER: Thank you, my good Noella.

NOELLA *disappears into the next room.*

THÉOPHILE: If you wish, we will offer a few invocations in his honour.

MOTHER: You're confident that Bruno will be acquitted, aren't you, Théophile?

THÉOPHILE: If it is God's holy will, yes, Auntie.

MOTHER: Good Catholics like us, He should be on our side, don't you think?

THÉOPHILE: Yes, Auntie—unless He grants you the grace of passing through the hard but sanctifying crucible of the ordeal.

MOTHER: Don't say that!

THÉOPHILE: Should this happen, ask Him for the strength to make your sacrifice willingly, like the model Christian you are.

MOTHER: Not today: I haven't the courage.

THÉOPHILE, *inexorable*: Just last Sunday, the Reverend
   Chaplain reminded us of the inspiring example of ev-
   angelical resignation offered by St. Agésilas of Corinth.

MOTHER, *expecting the worst*: What did he do?

THÉOPHILE: Without a single complaint he rotted for
   thirty-seven years in a dank dungeon—

MOTHER, *moaning*: St. Ann, St. Ann, save me!

THÉOPHILE:—to be granted finally the supreme consolation
   and crowning glory of martyrdom through decapitation.
   [*Over a last moan from the* MOTHER.] His venerated
   remains were cast into the public square and devoured
   by—

During THÉOPHILE'S *last speech, the curtain falls.*

ACT ONE

SCENE TWO

As the curtain rises, NOELLA *is on the telephone.*

NOELLA: Very well.... In about five minutes then? ...
Call from the lobby when you get here; I'll come right
down.... Listen, Albert: on the way back with Colette,
let's talk about something more cheerful than the trial,
shall we? Also, at home tonight, be nice and help me
avoid the subject in front of Papa and Mamma....
Thanks.... I don't know if he'll come, but I'll pass on
the invitation.... See you later. [*She hangs up.*]

Enter BOUSILLE, *out of breath.*

NOELLA: Hello, Bousille.

BOUSILLE: The others aren't here?

NOELLA: Not yet.

BOUSILLE: Good! I left Aurore and her mother at the
church. I would have liked to make the stations of the
cross, too, but I was afraid I'd miss the lawyer.

NOELLA: Don't worry. It's only five to six, and the appointment is for six-thirty.

BOUSILLE: Do you know if Colette is still coming?

NOELLA: I'm waiting for my brother; he's driving me to
pick her up.

BOUSILLE: You must be anxious to see her again?

NOELLA: Yes. I haven't seen her since Marc's death.

BOUSILLE: *He* was nice, too.

24

NOELLA: A fine boy, yes.

BOUSILLE: His mother must be heartbroken.

NOELLA: Not to mention that he was her sole support. [*In sympathy, and to change the subject, she notices that* BOUSILLE'S *right forefinger is wrapped in a handkerchief of doubtful cleanliness.*] You have cut yourself?

BOUSILLE: I feel sort of silly about it. There's a pet shop down the street, and, since I miss Fido, I stopped in for a moment to pat one of the dogs. I must have done something wrong: he bit my finger.

NOELLA: Let me see.

BOUSILLE, *taking off the makeshift bandage*: It wasn't his fault. The clerk said that whole breed is born with a bad temper.

NOELLA, *examining the finger*: It should be disinfected. Do you want me to apply a small dressing?

BOUSILLE: Do you have it here?

NOELLA: An old habit, from my nursing days. [*She takes a small first-aid kit from one of the bags.*] When I travel I always take along something for cuts and bruises. It can be useful, you see.

BOUSILLE: Yes, and that habit has already brought you happiness.

NOELLA: How's that?

BOUSILLE: You remember! You came to St. Tite for a weekend at Colette's, and Bruno introduced you to his brother, who had hurt his hand working on his bulldozer; you got out your kit and—the first thing you know—Henri and you were engaged!

NOELLA, *thoughtful for a moment*: Yes, the first thing I knew. . . . Give me your finger. [*She dabs iodine on* BOUSILLE'S *finger. He cannot repress a small shudder.*] It stings a little, doesn't it?

BOUSILLE: I'm such a cry-baby when it comes to physical pain.

NOELLA: Fido would never bite you.

BOUSILLE: That's for sure!

NOELLA: He's so good-tempered, poor fellow.

BOUSILLE: Even if you beat him, he'd never hold it against you.

NOELLA: He's a good dog, all right.

BOUSILLE: It seems to me the family doesn't appreciate him enough.

NOELLA: I'm afraid not. [*She has finished applying the dressing.*] There: it'll get better now.

BOUSILLE: Thank you, Noella.

NOELLA: You're losing a button. Give me your coat: I'll sew it back on.

BOUSILLE, *complying*: I'm not very stylish underneath.

NOELLA, *putting the first-aid articles back in the kit*: Do you still take those pills the doctor gave you?

BOUSILLE: Yes, every time my heart starts knocking a bit too hard.

NOELLA: Keep taking them and you'll live to be a hundred. [*She takes out a tiny sewing basket.*]

BOUSILLE: It's funny: whenever I come near you you do something kind for me.

NOELLA: It's only natural to help a nice boy like you.

BOUSILLE: I'm not as . . . nice as you think. It shows you're new in the family. Otherwise, you'd know I was addicted to the vice of drunkenness for nearly seven months and two weeks.

NOELLA: Did you go out with Bruno on his nights off to drink with him?

BOUSILLE: No—not at first, anyway—although I went with him for a very selfish reason. When I'm not helping someone I get so bored.

NOELLA: And you felt you were helping him?

BOUSILLE: His mother didn't worry so much when she

knew that I was there to drive the car back whenever Bruno . . . [*He hesitates.*]

NOELLA: Got drunk?

BOUSILLE: Yes. Mind you, she didn't always have cause to fret. Especially the nights when he was broke.

NOELLA: From what I can gather, it was Bruno who taught you to drink.

BOUSILLE: Well, you see, I started going with him two years ago, during the summer. As long as it was mild out I didn't mind waiting in the car. But when the cold weather came, I'd go inside the grill, now and then, to stick my feet under the radiator, and he'd shout: "Come and warm up, Bousille!" And he'd make me down two or three drinks, one after the other.

NOELLA: What for?

BOUSILLE: I guess it amused him to make me get up on the bar and dance a jig, once I lost track of what I was doing.

NOELLA: And after playing that stupid game long enough I suppose you realized one day you couldn't stop drinking?

BOUSILLE: It took less than a month. The taste for alcohol must have been in my blood—on account of my father, who loved it all his life.

NOELLA: You must have felt miserable.

BOUSILLE: I can't say it enough! What scared me most was the thought of dying crazy, like him. Especially since I'd lose my mind altogether when I'd had just a little too much. I'd imagine horrible devils chasing me around and I'd run through the village like an escaped lunatic.

NOELLA: That would be very bad for your heart.

BOUSILLE: Believe me, Noella, I'd rather be dead than fall back into that.

NOELLA: And how did you get out of such a hell?

BOUSILLE: Fortunately, one night when I was in no condition to replace him at the wheel, Bruno smashed the car against a tree, two miles out of St. Tite. He got off with a bruise on his forehead, but I spent six weeks with my knee in a cast and my leg strung up from the ceiling. That was my lucky break, as Father Sébastien used to say.

NOELLA: Who's Father Sébastien?

BOUSILLE: He's the one who got me out of that "hell," as you call it.

NOELLA: Really?

BOUSILLE: He came to see me every day, while I was in the hospital. That man is a real saint! He has such great faith that you feel . . . hypnotized when he speaks.

NOELLA: So you discussed your problem with him?

BOUSILLE: Yes, from beginning to end. He asked me: "Do you really want to stop drinking?" I said: "Yes, I do, Father, I do! I can't say it enough. But I'm always on my hands and knees." He said, "Of course, the temptation is stronger than you are because you're fighting it alone!" And then he proved it to me, in every possible way, that if I asked God—who is almighty—to fight on my side, that demon of the bottle could never, never defeat the both of us. Isn't that right?

NOELLA: No doubt about it.

BOUSILLE: I did what he told me: I put myself in the hands of God.

NOELLA: And you've never been tempted since?

BOUSILLE: Often. Nearly every time Phil hands me my little pay. But I don't worry.

NOELLA: Neither do I. I'm sure you'll always be able to resist.

BOUSILLE: I'm bound to: Father Sébastien guaranteed it to me: "As long as you don't fail God, have no worry. He won't fail you. He won't let you down, you can take my word for it." And he repeats that every time I see him.

NOELLA: If ever I meet your Father Sébastien, I'll kiss him on both cheeks. In the meantime, get back into your coat. [*She has brushed it, after sewing on the button.*]

BOUSILLE: Thank you, Noella. [*Putting on coat.*] That's why I'm so afraid of making a mistake in court tomorrow. What If I forgot something, after swearing solemnly to tell the whole truth? That would really be failing God. His second commandment!—three before the one where He forbids us to kill! Then He would let me fall back into my vice for sure.

The telephone rings.

And let me repeat it, Noella—

NOELLA, *answering the telephone*: Yes? . . . Very well, I'm coming right down. [*She hangs up.*]

BOUSILLE, *obsessed*: If that curse should strike me again, Noella, I'd rather be dead.

NOELLA, *getting ready to go out*: Don't worry, Bousille; everything will go well.

PHIL *comes in, followed by* HENRI. *Under his arm he carries a bottle of gin in a long brown paper bag.*

PHIL, *announcing*: Rejoice, children: Daddy's brought you a nice forty-ouncer! [*He puts the bottle down on the dresser and goes straight to the telephone.*]

HENRI, *to* NOELLA: What? You still around?

NOELLA: I was just leaving: Albert is waiting for me in the lobby.

HENRI: Get moving, damn it! The lawyer will be here in twenty minutes!

NOELLA: Don't worry; I'll be back with Colette at six-thirty, as arranged.

PHIL, *impatient, on telephone*: Hello!

NOELLA, *about to leave*: Mother has invited us to spend the evening in St. Lambert; will you come?

HENRI, *curtly, while looking for something in one of the bags*: No.

NOELLA: All right, then, I'll go alone. [*Exit.*]

PHIL, *on the telephone*: Hi, beautiful! A bucket of ice and three bottles of soda—sometime this year if possible —to the Royal Suite, 312! ... Thanks! [*He hangs up.*]

BOUSILLE, *to* HENRI: Then the lawyer is coming for sure?

HENRI: Yes. You'd better be here!

BOUSILLE: Count on me.

HENRI, *to* PHIL: Did you bring a clean shirt?

PHIL: Yes. Why?

HENRI: Let me have it. I'm soaking wet.

PHIL, *taking it out of one of the bags*: Okay.... But I wanted to get spruced up myself tonight.

HENRI: Hand it over! [*Snatches the shirt and goes into the next room to put it on.*]

BOUSILLE: Phil, do you think the trial went well today?

PHIL: I'll tell you that after the verdict.

BOUSILLE: The members of the jury have good honest faces, don't you think?

PHIL: Yes, they make a fine contrast with the judge's mug! [*He takes off his coat and loosens his tie.*]

BOUSILLE: What reassured me most was to see Bruno looking so calm all day.

PHIL, *lowering his voice so that* HENRI *cannot hear him*: No doubt about it, the kid pulls a good bluff!

BOUSILLE: He seemed upset, but not too much.

PHIL: Yeah! Just like a hockey player in the penalty box.

BOUSILLE: I'd sure like to be that relaxed when the time comes for me to face the judge.

PHIL: So, tomorrow's the day when you're ... presented at court?

BOUSILLE: First thing in the morning, yes; Aurore heard the lawyer tell Henri.

PHIL: I bet you can hardly wait, eh?

BOUSILLE: It makes me nervous; I can't say it enough!

PHIL: It's simple: just tell the truth. You're testifying, not making an election speech!

BOUSILLE: Joke all you want, but I'll give you absolute proof that a solemn oath, made on the Bible, should be taken seriously. Our neighbour on the left, when we lived outside the village, the year before I started school, a perfectly honest man until then—

PHIL: Quick! Tell me what happened; the suspense is killing me!

BOUSILLE: One election day he was offered five dollars to go to Shawinigan and vote in the name of a man who'd been dead for more than a year.

PHIL: Another crooked election!

BOUSILLE: Listen a minute: this is serious. So he presents himself at the poll; the scrutineer—

PHIL: Scrutinizes him closely.

BOUSILLE: Yes, and claims there's something fishy going on—

PHIL: Maybe a fellow from the other party beat him to it.

BOUSILLE: Maybe. Anyway, this poor man is trapped: no vote unless he takes an oath.

PHIL, *in mock horror*: How awful!

BOUSILLE: Whether he was afraid of being arrested or whether he didn't want to lose the five dollars, he yelled right out: "Bring me your Bible: I'll prove I've got the right to vote!"

PHIL: And he *did* swear?

BOUSILLE: Yes, my friend.

PHIL: There sure are some crooked people in the world!

BOUSILLE: Well, believe it or not, this same person, not more than three days later, while he was cutting fire-

31

wood—the right hand he had placed on the Bible to swear, by the very words of Christ, to tell the whole truth—zing! Into the buzz saw!

PHIL: Ouch! Mamma!

BOUSILLE: I was playing in the sand beside our house when I saw him—as plain as I see you now—burst into our place holding his bloody stump and screaming like a lost soul: "God has punished me! God has punished me!" Blood was gushing out all over! It was my father who applied a tourniquet and rushed him to the doctor at full speed.

PHIL: Poor fellow! Forced to button up with his left hand for the rest of his days!

BOUSILLE: After all, I might as well tell you, though I'm a little ashamed of it, that man was my uncle Oscar, my mother's brother.

PHIL: I always thought you were of noble descent!

BOUSILLE: Luckily my mother had died two years before: otherwise she would have been very upset. I was barely six at the time, yet I remember it as though it was only yesterday. For months I dreamt about blood running all over. I'd scream in the middle of the night: my grandmother had to wake me up. It was the next year that I had St. Vitus Dance.

PHIL: One secret for another, Bousille: I already knew your ... terrifying little tale.

BOUSILLE: You did?

HENRI, *returning from the next room*: Sure. Everybody knows the story of One-armed Oscar; for twenty years he blubbered it out in every beer parlour in the county. Every time you bought him a beer his stump would get three inches shorter.

There is a knock at the door.

BOUSILLE: That must be the lawyer.

PHIL: Come in!

The BELLBOY *enters with the ice and the soda water.*

PHIL: Ah! I've been waiting for this with my tongue hanging out! [*He tips the* BELLBOY.] Here, young man.

BELLBOY: Thank you, sir. [*He goes out.*]

PHIL, *offering* BOUSILLE *a drink*: You still refuse to join in our national sport?

BOUSILLE, *missing the joke*: No, thank you.

PHIL: I warn you: don't let yourself get rusty, boy. A pity you stopped: for a rookie of six months you stickhandled like a veteran. You were well on your way to the big league, you know.

BOUSILLE: Thank goodness Father Sébastien rescued me from that misery!

PHIL, *offering* HENRI *a glass as the latter reappears*: Here's to Father Sébastien!

BOUSILLE: If you're interested I can introduce you to him.

PHIL, *taking a drink*: Thanks a lot, but I'm happy the way I am.

HENRI, *putting down his glass*: I'm going to get the lawyer. [*Exit.*]

PHIL: Fine! [*To* BOUSILLE.] Say, is our dear mother-in-law still set on spending the night in St. Tite?

BOUSILLE: More than ever.

PHIL: Aurore, too?

BOUSILLE: She said something about going to look after the children, yes.

PHIL: Attaboy!

BOUSILLE: Are you coming too?

PHIL: No siree! It doesn't quite fit into my personal plans for the evening.

BOUSILLE: I'm still ready to drive them.

PHIL: You're a good boy. By the way, what about that flat we had this morning? Did you remember to get it fixed? [*He consults a pocket notebook.*]

BOUSILLE: Why—no.

PHIL: What are you waiting for?

BOUSILLE: I'm afraid of missing the lawyer.

PHIL: Bah! He won't be here for another **half-hour.** Lawyers are always late. [*On the telephone.*] Clairval 4-8367, please.

BOUSILLE: All right, but if he comes before I get back—

PHIL: Beat it, do you hear? I have to make a confidential call to . . . the President of the Children of Mary.

BOUSILLE: Oh! I see. [*He heads for the door, vaguely mystified.*]

PHIL, *on the telephone*: Hi there, baby!

BOUSILLE, *on his way out, looks back in surprise.*

PHIL: Come on now! This is your big bad wolf . . . Phil . . . Phil Vézina, from St. Tite. . . . Baby, your legs are long but your memory is short. . . . There! I thought you would . . . Sure, there's a real epidemic of amnesia these days. . . . Now, that's a lovely lie to hear. . . . Yes, I'm spending the night all alone in the big city and I'm afraid of getting wicked thoughts looking at T.V. Do you have room for me in your snug little love nest?. . . You're a doll! Let's say around nine. . . . Oh, and don't bother to invite your father and mother, eh?

AURORE *opens the door.*

AURORE, *shouting*: Phil! Give me a hand! Mamma fainted in the elevator. [*She dashes back out.*]

PHIL, *ending his call hastily*: I have to hang up. . . . See you at nine.

MOTHER, *coming in, supported by* AURORE *and the* BELL-BOY: Let go of me. I feel better now.

Exit the BELLBOY, *closing the door.*

AURORE: I told you to take it easy this afternoon.

PHIL: What's wrong, Mother dear?

AURORE, *helping her out of her coat*: You seem to do it on purpose, working yourself up like that! I warn you, I'll call the doctor if you keep this up.

MOTHER, *going into the bathroom*: Never mind the doctor.

AURORE: I don't want her to get another attack like the one she had two months ago. We have enough trouble as it is.

PHIL: Better get used to it. She'll be dying on our hands like this for another twenty years.

AURORE: I wonder if it's wise for her to go back to St. Tite for the night.

PHIL: Oh, sure! As long as you're making the trip with her there's no danger.

AURORE: I don't feel much like it, only—

PHIL: What about the children? It's all very well to be concerned about your brother, but we mustn't forget our duty as Christian parents.

AURORE: Are you coming, too?

PHIL: Well, no. I was just 'phoning Alphonse Major when you came in: I think he's about ripe to trade in his truck. If I could sell him a new one the money would come in handy now, with all the expenses of the trial.

AURORE: Well, I hope you're not going to take advantage of being alone to go out tomcatting!

PHIL: Are you kidding? We need God's help too much these days.

AURORE, *bursting out*: Yes, we certainly do! If ever we were caught like rats in a trap, this is it!

PHIL: Oh, I wouldn't say that!

AURORE: If it happened, my God, if it happened!

MOTHER, *coming out of the bathroom, a corset in her hands*: I feel better now. I wonder what came over me.

AURORE: To think that for years we've moved heaven

and earth so we could walk into a church with our heads
high—and now that big oaf gets us into this mess!

MOTHER: You know very well it wasn't his fault.

AURORE: No, maybe not!—since a bent twig makes a
crooked tree.

MOTHER: Now, don't start that again, Aurore.

AURORE: You gave in to his every whim, your little pet,
while the rest of us were brought up like dogs chained
to the dog-house.

MOTHER: When your father was alive—

AURORE: When Dad was alive, the only notice he took
of us was when he pulled off his belt and hit us over the
head with it. But I'd like to have seen anyone dare
touch a hair on dear little Bruno's head!

MOTHER: He was born five years after the rest of you,
poor child!

AURORE: That was no reason for spoiling him to the core.
Always down on your knees to him, as if he were the
Little Jesus of Prague!

MOTHER: Bruno is a good little boy, and you can't deny it.

AURORE, *pointing to the photograph*: Why don't you stop
seeing him in his first-communion suit? He took it off
fifteen years ago.

MOTHER: That's it: set yourself against him, all of you!
As if he didn't have enough trouble already!

AURORE: We're not against him. He's our brother; of
course we'll do everything we can to get him out of
this mess. We have no choice, [*Fuming.*] because if
he's convicted—

MOTHER: Don't say that: you'll kill me! [*Crying, she goes
to shut herself up in the next room.*]

AURORE: If he's convicted it's quite simple: we'll move
and never set foot in St. Tite again. I won't have the
children coming home from school in tears!

PHIL, *glass in hand*: Listen, Aurore, you're getting all worked up over nothing; there's no need to worry. The lawyer told us this morning—

HENRI *rushes in.*

HENRI: Shut your traps, damn it! They can hear you right down the hall.

PHIL: Let's close the transom; it's easier. [*He does so.*]

AURORE: Isn't the lawyer with you?

HENRI: He'll be right up. Went to park his car.

AURORE: It would have been more polite to wait for him down there.

HENRI: I know that as well as you do, but I wanted to see if Colette had arrived.

PHIL: Not yet. [*Offering him a drink.*] Are you thirsty?

HENRI: No, thanks. [*Preoccupied.*] She'd better show up.

AURORE: She could very well keep us waiting, that girl!

PHIL: Depend on Noella to see she gets here. *She* can be pretty stubborn, too.

There is a knock on the door.

AURORE: That's him! [*She hurriedly tidies up the room.*]

HENRI, *opening the door*: Come in.

The LAWYER *enters, briefcase in hand.*

HENRI: Make yourself at home.

LAWYER: Thank you.

HENRI: Colette Richard will be here any minute: my wife went to get her.

PHIL: As for Bousille, I just sent him on an errand. But he'll be trotting right back. I've never seen anyone so crazy about lawyers!

AURORE, *approaching*: Good evening, Mr. Fontaine.

LAWYER: Good evening.

37

AURORE, *to* HENRI: Mother had a weak spell just now.

HENRI: Again?

LAWYER: Nothing serious, I hope?

PHIL: When she gets excited the pressure goes up, the valves stick, and her motor conks out.

AURORE: She's all upset over Bruno, you know.

LAWYER: She shouldn't worry that much.

PHIL: No, because ... it seemed to me that everything went well today.

LAWYER: Today was just routine.

PHIL: The real battle starts tomorrow.

HENRI: Do you still think you'll be able to get an acquittal?

LAWYER: My opinion hasn't changed since this morning.

AURORE: Would you mind repeating that to Mother? It would cheer her up.

LAWYER: With pleasure. [*He follows* HENRI *into the next room.*]

PHIL, *nursing his drink*: Personally, Aurore, I have a feeling we'll win in a breeze.

AURORE: Of course, with a drink in your hand you men have no trouble seeing life through rose-coloured glasses!

The telephone rings.

PHIL, *answering*: Hello.... Yes, Noella.... Come right up; the lawyer is waiting. [*He hangs up.*] They're here.

AURORE, *nervously*: Let's promise a mass if everything goes well.

PHIL: Lay off the promises, you! I'm already stuck with seven years of penance!

AURORE: And try to be nice to the little bitch, so she won't play any dirty tricks on us.

HENRI, *opening the door and looking down the corridor*: Here she comes!

AURORE, *to the* LAWYER, *who is returning from the next room*: It's Colette. To soften her up, tell her that Bruno keeps asking about her all the time.

HENRI, *in the corridor*: Hello, Colette.

Ignoring him, COLETTE *comes in, followed by* NOELLA. *She is under a great nervous strain, which she tries to control.*

AURORE, *in honied tones*: Good afternoon, Colette dear! Or rather, good evening; at this hour we never know which to say. Let me take your coat.

COLETTE, *coldly*: No, thank you. I won't stay any longer than necessary.

HENRI: Colette, I'd like you to meet our lawyer, Mr. Fontaine.

LAWYER: How do you do, Miss Richard?

COLETTE *murmurs a vague acknowledgment.*

AURORE: Mr. Fontaine was just telling us that Bruno is always asking about you. He wants you to know he's dying to see you.

COLETTE: Even if it's true I couldn't care less. As far as I'm concerned, I hope I never see his face again.

MOTHER, *in her stocking feet, rushing in from the next room and throwing herself into* COLETTE'S *arms*: Colette, my sweet Colette! Isn't this terrible, eh? How you must be suffering, too! You loved him so much! We'll try to save him, all of us together.

HENRI, *cutting in*: Mother, you'd better get some rest if you want to go back to St. Tite tonight.

AURORE, *pressing the* MOTHER *back towards the other room*: And turn off your hearing aid, so we won't disturb you.

MOTHER: All right, but let me know when it's seven o'clock, for the Rosary programme on the radio.

39

AURORE: I promise.

MOTHER, *as she leaves*: We'll recite it as a family, eh, Colette?

AURORE *closes the door behind her.*

LAWYER: Won't you sit down, Miss Richard?

COLETTE *sits down and searches in her handbag nervously.*

PHIL: Cigarette, Colette?

COLETTE: No, thank you.

LAWYER: Miss Richard, first of all, I want to thank you for kindly agreeing to see me.

COLETTE: Don't mention it.

LAWYER: Even a brief knowledge of the testimony you will give tomorrow will help me better to serve the interests of the accused—and consequently—

COLETTE: Let's say that it will serve the interests of justice, period.

LAWYER: That's what I was about to add. If you'd rather see me privately, I could ask those present to withdraw.

COLETTE: Whether they leave or not, it's all the same to me. What I have to say I'd say in front of anybody. But let's hurry and get it over with.

LAWYER, *consulting a file*: I see here that your subpoena was delivered in Montreal, in care of Mr. Pierre—

COLETTE: He's my brother.

LAWYER: But, if my information is correct, at the time of the accident you were employed by the Astoria Café, in St. Tite?

COLETTE: Yes.

PHIL, *who can never resist the temptation to make a joke in order to relieve the tension*: Believe me, as a waitress, she gave you an appetite!

LAWYER: Mr. Gravel had been your friend for some time already, hadn't he?

AURORE, *forestalling her*: You met Bruno as soon as you came to town, eh, Colette? [*To the* LAWYER.] It'll be two years on All Saint's Day.

LAWYER: And during those two years, he courted you regularly?

COLETTE: "Courted" is a pretty big word.

LAWYER: In fact, everybody around you was aware that his intentions towards you were serious..

COLETTE: All the other fellows knew that I was his little "hands-off-whether-I-use-it-or-not." That's all.

LAWYER: Could one say that you were, in spirit if not in fact, engaged to each other?

COLETTE: Anyone is entitled to talk nonsense.

AURORE, *cutting in*: You weren't really, but I'd bet my last dollar he intended to clarify the situation very soon.

COLETTE, *between her teeth*: Oh, go climb a tree!

AURORE: He never gave you an engagement ring, we know, but—strictly between you and me and the bed-post, Colette—you have to admit that Bruno and you—

COLETTE: There are things that bind a boy and a girl more firmly that a four-dollar ring, sure enough. From that angle, you're right: we were engaged from our toes to our necks. Just the heads were left sticking out. The hearts, too.

LAWYER, *a bit nonplussed, trying to pick up the thread of his questioning*: Had the question of marriage ever come up, even casually, between the two of you?

COLETTE: Listen, Mr. Fontaine: you look like a lawyer with no time to waste. If anyone—here or elsewhere—has tried to make you believe that Bruno and I were a couple of perfect love-birds, don't let them kid you: Romeo and Juliet had their own way of wrestling with

41

each other; we had ours. As different as can be—to my great regret, believe me.

AURORE: Well, even if *you* couldn't stand him *he* was in love with you—head over heels!

COLETTE: If he adored me so much, he missed a wonderful chance to prove it last year, when he was scared stiff that our union had been "blessed." Instead of publishing the banns in church, His Lordship preferred to give me a bloody nose because I refused to spend a few days in Montreal to get the shipment side-tracked. Thank God it turned out to be a false alarm!

HENRI: Do you have any proof of this?

COLETTE: No. Except the envelope which Bruno shoved down the front of my dress, and which carried, in *your* finest handwriting, the address of the old witch I could go and see in perfect safety.

AURORE: Anybody with half a brain would understand that he couldn't afford to support a wife yet.

COLETTE, *more and more unnerved by all these interruptions from the family*: Of course not! Because, to support a wife, he would have had to get out of beer parlours and pool rooms and find a job.

HENRI: He *had* a job.

COLETTE, *to the* LAWYER, *sarcastically*: An insurance salesman, if you please! Once every two months, when somebody in the family needed to insure his car or his house he would oblige—provided the forms were brought for him to sign on the pin-ball machine.

LAWYER: If I understand correctly, Miss Richard, you claim you never loved the accused, in spite of the fact that for two years—

COLETTE: Oh, I had a crush on him—before I knew him —like every other girl who saw him flash by in the yellow convertible his brother-in-law, here present, sold him wholesale, thanks to his mother's money. But I soon had my eyes opened, when I realized he was nothing but a lazy drunken bum, who swiped the tips out of my purse to buy himself a bottle of booze whenever he was broke.

AURORE, *protesting*: Don't try and—

COLETTE: A jealous show-off, who thought he was the Sheik of Araby, and who expected me to thank him on both knees for the honour of belonging to his harem and amusing him, when there was nobody else around.

AURORE: If you were so disgusted with him, why did you keep on yowling around him, instead of dropping him?

COLETTE: Because he'd beat me black and blue every time I spoke of leaving him! Because I was so scared of him I couldn't sleep nights, knowing he was dangerous like all his jealous kind—particularly when he was drinking, which was seven nights a week.

HENRI: Colette, you'd better watch what you're saying—

COLETTE, *near the breaking point*: You keep your mouth shut, or I'll fix you, too! Sure, you're a good worker and you don't get drunk any more than most, but when it comes to playing the brute you can match your brother any time.

NOELLA: Colette!

COLETTE, *stopping, astonished at herself*: Forgive me, Noella. . . . I lost my head.

NOELLA: I understand, poor kid.

COLETTE: You know I wouldn't hurt you for anything in the world.

NOELLA: I know.

LAWYER, *making an effort to regain control of the situation*: If you don't mind, Miss Richard, we'll try to stick to the facts.

COLETTE: All right, but tell the others to stop butting in.

LAWYER: I was about to do so.

AURORE: After all, he is our brother! It seems to me we have a right to—

COLETTE: If you want to testify, you can yak-yak to your heart's content in court tomorrow. Right now I have the floor. And I don't want to have to tell you again. Or else I'll leave right now.

LAWYER, *alarmed*: I'm sure Mrs. Vézina understands that the interests of the accused—

AURORE: If you want me to leave, don't be shy about it.

COLETTE: Suit yourself; I'm not keeping you.

PHIL: Aurore, why don't you go and see if your mother needs you?

AURORE, *going into the other room, grumbling*: It's just so maddening to have someone lie right to your face, without even being able to—[*She slams the door.*]

Peace having returned, the LAWYER *gently leads* CO-LETTE *to a seat.*

LAWYER: I hope you agree, Miss Richard, that certain things, disclosed here today, need not be repeated before the court tomorrow.

COLETTE: I know. I'm not a fool.

LAWYER: It could profit no one, not even you.

COLETTE: If you don't question me about it, I won't bring it up.

LAWYER: You may depend on me.

BOUSILLE *comes in, breathless.*

BOUSILLE, *seeing the* LAWYER: Good evening, sir. I hope I didn't keep you waiting too long?

LAWYER: Not at all.

BOUSILLE, *nervously, to* PHIL: The fellow at the garage couldn't find the leak in the tire; I was on pins and needles! Believe it or not, it was a little nail no bigger than a baby's hair.

PHIL *signals him to be quiet, pointing to* COLETTE.

BOUSILLE, *seeing her for the first time*: Hello, Colette. [*He sits gingerly on the edge of a chair as she smiles at him.*] How are you? [*To* PHIL, *getting up again.*] Twenty-six pounds it takes in that tire, doesn't it?

PHIL, *annoyed*: Yes, yes!

BOUSILLE: Everything is ready. The car is parked right in front of—

HENRI, *curtly*: Okay! Shut up!

Crushed, BOUSILLE *resumes his seat and follows the ensuing interrogation raptly.*

LAWYER: May I take advantage of this interruption, Miss Richard, to remind you that you have been called as a witness for the Crown, as well as Mr.... [*He looks at* BOUSILLE, *trying to remember his name.*]

BOUSILLE, *whispering*: Belzile.

LAWYER: Thank you. I'll question you only in the cross-examination—and if I deem it advisable.

AURORE, *inevitably, creeps back in and listens, closing the door behind her and resting against the door jamb.*

LAWYER, *after a short silence*: Marc Lepage, the victim, had known you for a long time?

COLETTE, *bowing her head*: I met him at Easter, at Noella's engagement party, in St. Lambert. [*Her former harshness gives away to melancholy.*]

LAWYER: He'd simply been introduced to you?

COLETTE: I danced with him nearly all evening.

LAWYER: Was Bruno Gravel your escort at this party?

COLETTE: Let's say he was an escort to the bottle, along with the other men in the kitchen.

LAWYER: He didn't object to the attentions Marc Lepage paid to you?

45

COLETTE: In the middle of the party he came over—between drinks—and told me to stop dancing.

LAWYER: Did you comply with his request?

COLETTE: No.

LAWYER: You went on dancing, knowing that your behaviour was displeasing to him?

COLETTE, *upset*: I couldn't help it. For the first time in my life I was being treated like a princess. I thought I was dreaming. [*She suppresses a sob in her handkerchief. After a silence.*] Excuse me.

LAWYER: Later that evening did Bruno rebuke you in any way?

COLETTE: Not that night, no. Aurore can tell you why just as well as I can.

AURORE, *ill at ease*: Lots of people get sick after a party.

COLETTE: Meaning he came back to St. Tite dead drunk in the back of the car.

LAWYER: From that time until the day of Mr. and Mrs. Gravel's wedding, was there ever any mention of the victim between Bruno and yourself?

COLETTE, *after hesitating*: If it's important to the case, I'll answer. If not, I'll tell you it's my own business.

LAWYER: You are not obliged to answer, of course, but the element of provocation is very important in a case of this kind. I'm honestly trying to determine to what extent the accused was provoked by the advances of a rival. Any reticence on your part before the court in this respect—

NOELLA: Go ahead, Colette. I don't care any more.

COLETTE, *after a slight pause*: A week after the party, I went to Noella's room one evening to help her pack. She was leaving the next day to get her trousseau ready.

LAWYER: At her parents' house?

COLETTE: Yes. After making me promise to tell no one, she handed me a letter Marc had sent her for me. He

46

wrote that for him Lent had begun that Easter evening when we parted, and he had been thinking of me ever since. Later that night, Bruno came to the room and found the letter, when he snitched a package of cigarettes from my coat pocket.

LAWYER: What was his reaction?

COLETTE: He slapped me so much I was nearly fainting when Noella managed to stop him.

LAWYER, *after reflecting briefly*: Allow me to emphasize this point: did the accused—that evening or at any other time—make threats against Marc Lepage in any way?

COLETTE: No. But he promised to break *my* neck if Marc ever came near me. That would be easier.

LAWYER, *relieved*: Thank you. Did you expect Marc Lepage to attend your friend's wedding?

COLETTE: Noella had invited him, but he wasn't sure that he would get the day off.

LAWYER, *realizing his question is painful*: Now, can you tell me what you know about the accident which happened to him that day—and the circumstances that led up to it?

COLETTE, *almost inaudibly, burying her face in her hands*: I can't. . . . Ask Bousille; he knows more about it than I do.

BOUSILLE, *nervously, as the* LAWYER *turns toward him*: The night before last I wrote out a little account of what I did that day, hour by hour: do you think it would be illegal for me to use it? [*He indicates a few sheets of cheap paper in his hands.*]

LAWYER: No, if it can be of help to you.

BOUSILLE, *earnestly*: I want so much to tell the truth, the whole truth, and nothing but the truth.

LAWYER, *smiling reassuringly*: I'm sure you will. You were present at the wedding from the morning on, weren't you?

BOUSILLE, *pouring out the words in a rush*: Exactly, yes. At first, I wasn't supposed to come because I didn't have enough money for a wedding gift. But Henri was very kind; he said to me: "Come anyway. That will give you a chance to drive my car back." You see, the newlyweds were going on their honeymoon by 'plane, so someone had to return the car from the airport to St. Tite. Besides, Bruno's mother had asked me to keep an eye on him, as usual, in case he might tend to . . . get a little high.

LAWYER: Did he get . . . high?

BOUSILLE, *unhappily*: Well . . . I'd be rather inclined to say yes, . . . since, around noon, he could hardly stand alone on his feet.

LAWYER: Up till then you had followed him pretty closely?

BOUSILLE: Oh, I never let him out of my sight. But I can't say it was exhausting work: he stuck to the hotel bar most of the time.

LAWYER: Can you give me any idea of the quantity of alcohol he had consumed since morning?

BOUSILLE, *after a moment of serious reflection*: I'd say . . . about three glasses of wine . . . and four or five double scotches. . . . That was over and above the thirteen ounces he swallowed in the car on the way to St. Lambert.

LAWYER: Had he eaten before leaving St. Tite?

BOUSILLE: Not that I know of. Eh, Aurore? [*She shrugs.*] He was late getting up because he and a few friends had thrown a farewell stag party the night before in Shawinigan. Henri wasn't there, but they gave him a send-off anyway.

LAWYER: So, you were saying that around noon—

BOUSILLE: I went over to Phil's table and whispered the facts in his ear. He whispered right back: "Get him a room upstairs and let him sleep the sleep of the just."

LAWYER: That's what you did?

BOUSILLE: Yes.

LAWYER, *trying to cut it short*: And you kept an eye on him while he slept until four o'clock?

BOUSILLE, *after checking his notes*: Except that, for a moment, I fell asleep too in my chair: it was warm in the room, you see, and I had been up since dawn.

LAWYER: And when you woke up?

BOUSILLE: I realized I was starving—a little. So I tiptoed out of the room and asked the clerk at the desk: "Can I get a good hot-dog around here—not too expensive?" He answered: "Why don't you go to the Alice Barbecue, over there?" Just as I got to the restaurant, I bumped into Colette and Marc, who were also coming in for a bite.

LAWYER: They had spent the afternoon together?

BOUSILLE: Apparently, yes. Eh, Colette?

LAWYER: Go on.

BOUSILLE, *resuming halfheartedly*: So the three of us went in. I was going to sit at the counter, but Marc called out to me: "Come and join us." I said: "No, thank you, I'd disturb you. Besides, a full-course meal at a table is too expensive for me." But he insisted: "Come on, be my guest. We need a chaperone." He and Colette grabbed me by both arms and we danced between the tables to a little corner in the back. They were as happy as children, the two of them.

LAWYER: You were the only ones in the restaurant?

BOUSILLE: Except for the owner, yes. Then Marc said to her: "Madame Alice Barbecue, you have three happy customers in front of you. The only trouble is that they are as hungry as wolves. Can you do anything about that?" She replied: "You bet I can!" Just as she disappeared into the kitchen with our order, bang! We heard the restaurant door slam. [*He stops, miserable.*] Do you want to go on from there, Colette?

COLETTE, *in tears, shakes her head. Short of breath,*

BOUSILLE *takes a small bottle from his pocket and swallows a pill unobtrusively.*

LAWYER: I'll help you. It was Bruno who had just come in?

BOUSILLE, *nodding*: The clerk at the hotel must have told him where I went.

LAWYER: He came up to the table and ordered Colette to leave with him, but she refused, didn't she?

BOUSILLE: Yes. Bruno grabbed her wrist, shouting: "Come here, you! You heard me the first time!"

LAWYER: That's when Marc intervened?

BOUSILLE: He gave Bruno a shove in the stomach.

LAWYER: Bruno lost his balance and the water from the glass in Colette's hand splashed in his face, didn't it?

BOUSILLE: Exactly. As he got up, gasping for breath, I jumped in front of him: "Bruno, don't be a fool," I said. "Come and dry yourself off."

LAWYER: And you succeeded in pulling him away?

BOUSILLE: I got him into the men's room, which was right near.

LAWYER: Tell me what happened there.

BOUSILLE, *unhappy*: I had just helped Bruno out of his coat to dry it when Marc came in.

LAWYER: Did Miss Richard see what went on then?

BOUSILLE: No. I was the only witness, unfortunately, since the door closed by itself. It was a spring door, you see.

LAWYER: Go on.

BOUSILLE: I thought Marc had come to apologize, because he held out his hand and said: "Listen, Gravel, on a nice day like this we're not going to—" He never finished: Bruno gave him a punch right square on the jaw. [*Painfully*.] Marc fell backwards. His head banged on the cement floor—

COLETTE *is nearly ill into her handkerchief.* NOELLA *leads her into the bathroom.*

AURORE: Bruno must have figured Marc was going to start in on him again and decided to get in the first punch. It's quite clear.

LAWYER, *to* BOUSILLE: Is that really all that took place?

BOUSILLE: Until then, yes. [*Showing his paper.*] What followed may not be important, but—

LAWYER: Am I to understand that the fight wasn't over after Marc fell?

BOUSILLE: Well.... Marc tried to get up, as if he were drunk: he was moaning and holding his head in his hands. That's when Bruno grabbed him by the shirt and lunged at him to hit him again, saying: "This one is for your damned letter to Colette. And I've been saving it for you for two months." I hardly had time to grab his wrist and make him miss.

HENRI, *advancing towards him*: What's this you're dreaming up?

BOUSILLE: Then I jumped on him and tried to hold on till the others came.

LAWYER, *after a moment of general amazement, leafing through his file*: I don't find these last details in the statement you gave at the inquest.

BOUSILLE: No, that's just it. [*He stumbles, unnerved.*] You see, ... the inquest was held the next day.... I could hardly speak: I was shaking like a leaf. As you all know, while I was describing the first blow I passed out and the doctor had to give me an injection for my heart. When I recovered my senses, the coroner was gone.

LAWYER: Of course, the evidence already obtained warranted the arrest of the accused.

BOUSILLE: And nobody ever asked me about it since. That's why I was so anxious to talk to you, to find out if, according to the law, I still have the right to—

The telephone rings. AURORE *answers it.*

LAWYER: You cannot contradict your testimony, but nothing can prevent you from completing it, of course.

COLETTE, *supported by* NOELLA, *has just come out of the bathroom.*

AURORE, *hanging up*: Noella's brother is here to pick up Colette. He's waiting for her in the lobby.

COLETTE, *in a weak voice*: I'm going down. [*To the* LAWYER.] It that all?

LAWYER: Yes, Miss Richard. Once again, I thank you— for myself and on behalf of the accused.

COLETTE, *holding back her tears*: So much the better if what I told you can spare him the punishment he deserves ... for killing a poor boy who was ready to love me ... even if I wasn't worth it. [*She heads for the door.*]

NOELLA: I'll take you down.

COLETTE: Don't bother.

NOELLA: Please let me. [*Exeunt.*]

AURORE: It remains to be seen whether she'll tell the truth tomorrow. I'd swear she hasn't received holy communion for at least two years!

LAWYER, *thoughtful*: It isn't *her* testimony that worries me. [*To* BOUSILLE.] So, you were saying that when he attempted a second blow—which, incidentally, you were able to deflect—Bruno clearly stated: "This one is for your damned letter to Colette—"

BOUSILLE, *finishing the sentence*: "And I've been saving it up for you for two months."

LAWYER, *after a short pause*: Thank you.

BOUSILLE, *uneasy in the frozen silence*: Could that have any serious effect?

LAWYER, *to himself as much as to the others*: The prosecution will certainly insist on that point to prove premeditation on the part of the accused. Under such conditions, it will be difficult, if not impossible, for me to get the case dismissed, as I had hoped.

AURORE, *stubbornly*: Personally, I don't see what difference it makes.

LAWYER: As I told you this morning, I intended to plead legitimate self-defence.

AURORE: Of course.

NOELLA *comes back into the room.*

LAWYER: How can I maintain such a position now if it was proven in court—through the incident just related by Mr. Belzile—that your brother had been fully determined, for at least two months, to attack Marc Lepage?

HENRI: Which means, in plain words, he may be convicted?

LAWYER: I'm afraid so.

AURORE: God help us!

LAWYER: However, you shouldn't be overly alarmed. I still hope to convince the jury that at worse this is an affair of passion, involving an accused without any previous police record, who obviously had no intention of killing his rival, even if he meant to give him a thrashing.

PHIL: What sentence is he liable to get?

LAWYER: Five or six months. He may even get off with the time already spent in jail.

AURORE, *desperately*: But that's not what we wanted! If he's found guilty he'll be a jail bird for the rest of his life. On the other hand, if he's exonerated of all guilt, as you said this morning—

LAWYER: My dear Mrs. Vézina, my duty is to defend

the accused by every legal means at my disposal, but even so I cannot alter the testimony of a witness.

BOUSILLE, *visibly tired, wiping his brow*: Please ... are you through with me?

LAWYER: For the time being yes.

BOUSILLE: Then may I go and get a drink of water?

LAWYER: Of course.

BOUSILLE: Thank you. [*He goes into the bathroom.*]

LAWYER, *glancing at his watch*: You'll excuse me for leaving now: I must go.

AURORE, *not giving up*: I hope you are still convinced of Bruno's innocence, in spite of what that half-wit babbled to you?

LAWYER, *closing his briefcase*: My personal convictions are less important than the conclusions the jury will arrive at tomorrow.

AURORE: Who knows if he didn't dream up half what he said? A reformed drunk, who used to get delirious the minute he hit the bottle!

LAWYER: I can only repeat that, in any case, I will do my utmost to obtain a verdict of Not Guilty, even if I have little hope of succeeding.

HENRI: I, in the meantime, will try to clear the matter up with Bousille.

PHIL: We must make sure that he tells the truth and nothing but the truth, as he says he wants to.

LAWYER, *politely*: Obviously. [*As* AURORE *gives him his hat.*] Goodbye, ladies ... and gentlemen. [*Exit.*]

AURORE, *the minute the door closes, looking straight into* HENRI'S *eyes; in a low voice*: Are you thinking what I'm thinking?

HENRI'S *silence indicates agreement.*

PHIL, *coming nearer*: Apparently, we all three have the same inspiration.

HENRI, *after a pause*: He's driving you to St. Tite later?

AURORE: Yes.

HENRI: Don't forget to bring him back to me early to-morrow morning.

AURORE: Wouldn't you rather take the ... sheep by the horns right away?

HENRI: I won't give *him* the chance to sleep on the idea.

PHIL, *watch in hand*: Besides, if you don't want to get there too late you'd better get a move on: it's already five past seven.

AURORE, *starting*: My God! I promised Mamma to wake her up at seven without fail.

NOELLA, *who has been listening in dismay, going to* HENRI: I hope I misunderstood.... I hope you don't really mean to—

HENRI, *cutting her off brutally, as* BOUSILLE *comes out of the bathroom*: Mind your own business!

BOUSILLE, *conscious of his delicate position, trying to put on a good face*: The lawyer's gone? He has an honest face, don't you think? We are lucky, in our misfortune, to have—

HENRI: Come here, you.... [*He motions* BOUSILLE *to come closer and fixes him with a stare.*] About the ending of your story just now, are you sure you got it straight?

BOUSILLE, *transparent*: Of course.

HENRI: Turn it over in your mind, on your way back home.

BOUSILLE: I can think about it again, but I don't see what good it would—

HENRI, *slapping him lightly and quickly*: Just think it over, okay? And we'll discuss it tomorrow morning.

MOTHER, *bursting into the room in her stocking feet and turning on the radio*: Quick, everybody: on your knees! The Family Rosary has started on the radio!

[*She drops to her knees herself.* AURORE *is about to do the same and looks for her beads in her handbag.* HENRI *is still standing, his eyes holding* BOUSILLE'S. *The* MOTHER, *meanwhile, is chanting.*] Good St. Ann, we'll recite this rosary in your honour. See to it that our dear little Bruno is proclaimed innocent!

AURORE, *about to kneel, seeing* PHIL *peacefully finishing his drink, and slapping him on the back*: On your knees, you!

MOTHER, *continuing, while* NOELLA, *in the background, looks on, her face grim*: You alone can save him, good St. Ann! If you answer my prayer, I promise you we'll go on a nice pilgrimage, with the whole family!

During her last speech, the curtain falls.

ACT TWO

SCENE ONE

A grey morning light filters through the venetian blind. Alone on stage, PHIL *is lying on the bed snoring, still dressed in his pants, shirt and socks. At the first ring of the telephone, he turns over. It rings again.*

PHIL, *still half asleep, mumbling*: Henri! . . . The 'phone!

> NOELLA, *in her slip, comes from the next room and answers.*

NOELLA: Hello? . . . No, he's not here. . . . I don't know. . . . Yes. Do you want to speak to him? [*She puts down the receiver.*] Phil! [*She comes to him and shakes him.*] Phil, it's Aurore.

PHIL, *startled, wide awake*: Aurore? Where?

NOELLA: On the 'phone. [*She goes back to the next room, as Phil comes to the telephone, yawning.*]

PHIL, *pulling himself together as he takes the receiver*: Hello, Kitten! . . . Oh, no! . . . I've been up for two solid hours—about . . . Henri? He must be having breakfast. He was already gone when I woke up. Where are you calling from? . . . Yeah! . . . Well, get the number of the other car, that's all you can do: the insurance will pay—

> HENRI *comes in.*

PHIL, *going on*: No damage on your side? . . . Good! Hold

on a second, Henri's just coming in. [*To* HENRI.] Bousille dented a fender, near Lafontaine Park—

HENRI, *snatching the receiver*: What the hell are you doing? ... Cut the gab and get here on the double with him; it's already five past nine! Understand? [*He hangs up with a bang.*]

PHIL, *hurriedly making himself presentable*: Boy, Aurore sure came close to catching me in bed that time! Lucky I was sleeping alone. I hope I didn't wake you up when I came in this morning—er, I mean, last night?

HENRI, *pouring himself a drink*: Do you take me for a dope? You were banging on the door with your fists: I'm the one who let you in.

PHIL: Oh, yes, of course! It's terrible how my memory slips as I get older. You see, I went to visit one of my cousins. [*Unruffled by* HENRI'S *brief but significant look.*] He produced a bottle; we started talking about the good old days. Boy, did we have a ball! When we came back to earth it was daybreak. And you, how did *you* relax your weary bones?

HENRI, *his thoughts elsewhere*: I had a few beers in the bar downstairs.

PHIL: Noella?

HENRI: With her family.

PHIL, *coming towards him*: By the way, no need to mention this to Aurore, eh?

HENRI: What?

PHIL: About me getting back a bit late. You know her: I can tell her the honest-to-God truth till I'm blue in the face—

HENRI: I don't give a damn. I've got other fish to fry today.

PHIL: Thanks. I'll do the same for you someday. A wolf like you, I'm pretty sure—[*He stops suddenly, as* NO-ELLA *comes in to straighten the bed.*]

PHIL, *now ready to go out*: I'm going downstairs a few minutes to fill up with black coffee.

HENRI: Get your coffee, but come back here to drink it. Bousille will be in any minute and I need your help to put the screws on.

PHIL, *worried*: Still got the same idea in your block?

HENRI: Do what you're told!

PHIL, *almost serious*: On that particular subject, you know, my convictions are not too firm this morning. I spent the whole night meditating on the problem, and—

HENRI, *raising his voice*: Scram, damn it, if you want to get back!

PHIL: Okay! Okay! Relax: you know it takes you less than that to start me shaking in my shoes. [*Exit.*]

NOELLA, *after a silence*: I must speak to you, Henri, and what I have to say is very serious. Try to listen to me for once. [*She has come towards him.*] You've got to forget your scheme about Bousille.

HENRI, *going on drinking, without even looking at her*: I told you last night to keep your nose out of this.

NOELLA: With him it would be too pitiful. You'd have no excuse—and you know why.

HENRI: Mind your own damn' business, you hear?

NOELLA: I've asked so little of you until now; do me this one favour.

HENRI, *turning towards her, his eyes hard*: You'd better not get in my way.

NOELLA: I need so badly to keep a little respect for you.

HENRI: You'd be sorry for a long time, baby.

NOELLA: I beg you, Henri.

HENRI: And get this: I don't want you around when I talk to him. Do what you like, but beat it—understand?

PHIL *comes in.*

PHIL: I've brought you a guest!

59

Brother THÉOPHILE *enters, hat in hand, as* NOELLA *returns to the next room.*

PHIL: We met in the elevator.

THÉOPHILE: Good morning, Henri. I hope I'm not disturbing you too much?

PHIL: I was just telling him that perhaps this isn't the ideal time for—

HENRI, *drily*: No, it's not the time.

THÉOPHILE, *stammering*: I came to Bonsecours Market with the Brother Cook, so—

HENRI: You want to see Bousille?

THÉOPHILE: Yes, I would like to—

HENRI: He's not here.

THÉOPHILE: I only saw him for a few moments yesterday, so—

PHIL, *cutting in*: But he'll be here any minute—

THÉOPHILE: Then I'll wait for him in the lobby, just to say "Hello"—

HENRI, *firmly*: No, you will not! I've got business with him.

THÉOPHILE, *retreating, more and more ill at ease*: Very well, then.... [*To* PHIL.] By the way, will you tell Aunt Gravel that this morning at high mass Bruno was recommended to our prayers?

PHIL, *tongue in cheek*: You can be sure she'll leap for joy.

THÉOPHILE, *too lost in shyness to feel* PHIL's *dry humour*: And kindly let her know that this afternoon about three o'clock I'll be around again to comfort her.

PHIL: About three? Swell! She'll have her handkerchief ready.

THÉOPHILE, *taking leave*: Till then, be of good faith!

PHIL: Thanks, old man!

AURORE *bursts in like a whirlwind as* THÉOPHILE *leaves.*

AURORE: Whew! [*She drops into a chair, out of breath.*]

PHIL, *kissing her on the cheek*: Hello, Kitten! Your big bad wolf was lonesome for you.

HENRI: Damn it! This is a fine time to get here.

AURORE, *at the breaking point*: Don't you bawl me out! I'm upset enough as it is.

PHIL: You had a hell of a trip, didn't you?

AURORE: You said it! On top of that, I didn't sleep a wink till daybreak.

PHIL, *disgusted with life*: Me neither: tossing and turning all night!

AURORE: I thought we'd never get here! With Bousille crawling along at thirty miles an hour, claiming he was seeing double!

HENRI: Where is he?

AURORE: In the car with Mamma. He doesn't want to come up right away.

HENRI, *to* PHIL: Go and get him. And drag him back by the scruff of the neck, if you have to.

PHIL: Okay. [*He leaves, unhappy.*]

AURORE: If you don't need me, I'll go along with Mamma to catch what's left of the nine o'clock mass at Notre Dame. I'll see you at the Court House.

HENRI: As you like.

AURORE, *about to leave*: His car accident with Bruno, when did it happen?

HENRI: A year ago last Labour Day.

AURORE: How much time did he have to start an action for damages?

HENRI: One year.

AURORE: Then there's no more worry he'll cause us trouble on that score?

HENRI: No danger! He'd be too stupid to sue, even if he had another ten years to do it.

61

AURORE: Good luck! [*She pats his arm.*] I'll pray for your success. [*Exit.*]

HENRI *pours himself a drink at the dresser, as* NOELLA *comes out of the next room, ready to leave.*

HENRI, *approaching her*: All the same, you'll tell me where you're going.

NOELLA: I too am going to pray—that justice be done. Then I'll come back and take care of your mother, while you're all over there.

Enter PHIL, *followed by* BOUSILLE.

PHIL: Come in, Bousille; don't be shy.

BOUSILLE, *to* NOELLA, *who approaches him and looks at him sadly*: You're leaving Noella?

NOELLA: Yes, poor boy. [*She kisses his cheek and leaves, without another word.*]

BOUSILLE, *lingering shyly at the door*: You know, Phil, I'm sorry about the car. Maybe it was the rain that blurred my eyes.

PHIL: Am I blaming you?

BOUSILLE: No, but it worries me like the devil.

PHIL: Anybody can make a mistake.

HENRI, *cutting in*: What's really bad is refusing to admit it when you've made one. You agree?

BOUSILLE: Sure.

HENRI, *under* BOUSILLE'S *nose*: Now get this: you can forgive a man anything, when he's ready to admit he's wrong.

BOUSILLE: Yet, I'm sure I looked carefully before turning left—

PHIL: Forget it. Sentence suspended.

HENRI: Take off your raincoat; you're liable to get pretty warm in here.

BOUSILLE, *ill at ease*: No, thank you: I shouldn't mind attending a little bit of mass myself, with Aurore and—

HENRI: Take it off, I tell you.

BOUSILLE: It's the feast of the Holy Guardian Angels today.... So, ... in view of the circumstances—

HENRI, *unable to repress a movement of impatience*: Will you listen to me, damn it!

PHIL, *joking to reassure* BOUSILLE: You have two guardian angels right here! [*He helps him out of his raincoat.*]

HENRI: Sit down. Let's talk for a couple of minutes. [*He makes him take a chair.*]

PHIL, *removing the prayer-book from* BOUSILLE'S *hands*: May I relieve you of your library?

BOUSILLE: It's a gift from Father Sébastien.

PHIL: Yeah! When you've got your nose in this I bet you don't see the collection plate when it goes by, eh?

BOUSILLE: Frankly, I find it very useful.

PHIL, *trying to delay* HENRI'S *attack*: So, what's new in St. Tite?

BOUSILLE: Oh, I can tell you, the dog was glad to see me.

PHIL: Well, that's hardly news!

BOUSILLE, *his heart warmed*: He was so happy, the poor fellow! He was jumping this high!

PHIL: As I was pointing out to Aurore the other night, there's an amazing affinity between your two personalities.

BOUSILLE: He's such a good dog.

PHIL: No doubt about it, he's a very refined character. But I think he runs around a bit too much for his strength.

BOUSILLE: It worries me, too. With his rheumatism—

PHIL: He's just at the age when an over-ambitious dog can strain his back.

BOUSILLE: He should rest more, that's for sure.

PHIL: Why don't you try and make him understand, in a tactful way?

HENRI, *bursting out, unable to stand it any longer*: Okay! But right now we have better things to discuss than Fido's change of life!

PHIL, *grumbling, before stepping aside*: What's wrong with discussing the problems of a mutual friend for two minutes?

HENRI, *after pausing to flip the page morally*: Cigarette?

BOUSILLE: No, thank you. It upsets my stomach when it's empty.

HENRI, *studying him covertly*: A hell of a thing, this trial, eh, Bousille?

BOUSILLE: You're so right! I couldn't close my eyes all night thinking about it.

HENRI: Yes, a hell of a thing.

BOUSILLE: But, from what the lawyer said yesterday, Bruno stands a chance of coming out of it not too badly, after all.

HENRI: Bah! He was only trying to brighten up a dark picture. I hope you were smart enough to catch on.

BOUSILLE: Frankly, no.

HENRI: I'll tell you straight, at the risk of upsetting you: the way the gears are shifting, Bruno could take a five-year trip to the penitentiary, just like that.

BOUSILLE: You think so?

HENRI: Anything can happen. A judge on the Bench, my friend, is just as unpredictable as a referee in the ring. He only has to dislike your mug—and you've had it!

PHIL: That's for sure!

HENRI: It would be a cruel blow for the family. I wonder if Mother would get over it.

PHIL: With the pressure she's got in her boiler, I wouldn't answer for it.

BOUSILLE: That would be a shame.

HENRI: There's a woman who loves you a lot! I can assure you of that.

BOUSILLE: Oh, I know she does. I'm fond of her, too.

HENRI: And you should be, after all she's done for you.

BOUSILLE: Naturally.

HENRI: I hope you will never cause her any grief.

BOUSILLE: That would be pretty mean of me.

HENRI: Let's face it: you'd be an ingrate.

BOUSILLE: She grumbles at me, sometimes, but—

HENRI: Your own mother would do the same.

BOUSILLE: Maybe. I hardly knew her: she was buried when I was only four.

HENRI: That's why you are practically our little adopted brother.

BOUSILLE: Oh, I'd be even more alone without you all, of course.

HENRI: Take Bruno, for instance. That guy couldn't make a move without you.

BOUSILLE, *without malice*: Some nights, especially.

PHIL: Even the children at home, do you realize how much they have taken you to their little hearts? When we go out at night and tell them you're going to baby-sit with them again, they simply dance for joy!

BOUSILLE, *touched*: Honestly?

PHIL: They love you! Why, let me confess it, as their own father I'm sometimes jealous of you.

BOUSILLE: I'm so glad to hear you say that. I think they're nice, too, but it seemed to me that ... [*He hesitates.*]

PHIL: What?

BOUSILLE: ... They laughed at me behind my back, now and then.

PHIL: Where the devil did you get an idea like that? Holy cow, you're full of complexes! Isn't it sad, eh, Henri? A well-balanced guy like him, a fine education, a whole year of culture at the Brothers' after third grade, tormenting himself like that!

HENRI: Particularly when the entire family goes out of its way to show him consideration.

BOUSILLE: It's not your fault.

PHIL: I should say not!

BOUSILLE: I must be suspicious by nature: ever since I was so high I've been scared of getting jabbed in the back with a pitchfork.

HENRI: Come off it: your father's been dead a long time. And they took the pitchfork out of his hands before they closed the coffin.

BOUSILLE, *to* HENRI: It's funny, but you remind me of him, sometimes.

HENRI: *I* remind you of your father?

BOUSILLE: Well ... I mean ...

PHIL: Don't tell me this nice guy scares you?

BOUSILLE: Not always.

PHIL: He looks like a bull at first glance, but scratch the hide a bit: you'll find the meat is very tender underneath.

HENRI, *sitting down next to* BOUSILLE: I'll tell you in two words what I'm like: you've often seen me riding my bulldozer when I'm levelling ground, haven't you?

BOUSILLE, *with conviction*: You're so impressive! You're not sitting on the bulldozer; you *are* the bulldozer, it seems.

HENRI: You can say that again. As long as I'm working in soft ground, I take it easy—listen to the little birds sing. But if a stump or a pile of rocks gets in my way, then suddenly I see red: I lower my horns and I charge! And everything smashes down in front of me.

PHIL: A real tornado!

BOUSILLE: I know: it gives you the goose pimples. Remember the nice poplar, with the garden swing under it, near the house? Noella liked to sit out there, in the shade, knitting or mending your overalls—

HENRI, *to* PHIL: He has quite a memory, hasn't he? Just like an elephant!

BOUSILLE: Well, one fine morning last summer—I still wonder what bit you during the night—you burst out of the house half-dressed, with your braces hanging down, you jumped on your bulldozer and—wham!— sent the tree crashing into the field and smashed the swing to smithereens!

HENRI, *staring into* BOUSILLE'S *eyes*: Nobody should cross me, see? Nobody should get in my way; that's the whole point. Understand?

BOUSILLE: It's clear.

HENRI: But when people agree with me, why then I can be as good and big-hearted as anybody! You want proof? Remember when you came out of hospital, after your car accident with Bruno? Forty days of treatment, plus room and board! How much did it come to?

BOUSILLE, *crestfallen*: Four hundred and ninety-two dollars, and sixty-five cents—including the X-rays.

HENRI: A small fortune, eh? Who was the mean guy who bled himself white to pay that bill for you?

BOUSILLE: I often wondered how the Reverend Sister Bursar had the nerve to send it to you, especially since I'd already heard her tell the doctor that "a certain individual had serious responsibilities in this affair." If she was right, it seems to me that *he* might have helped me temporarily, not you.

HENRI: You poor sap! Don't you realize yet that this individual could have been Bruno, or me, or any one of us?

BOUSILLE, *in all simplicity*: No.

HENRI: Responsibilities? Sure we had some! And serious ones, too! You're part of the family, aren't you?

BOUSILLE: It's very kind of you to say so.

67

HENRI:　When your brother, through his own fault or not, falls into a sewer up to his chin, you have no choice: it's your duty to hold your nose and pull him out of there before he swallows too much. Right?

BOUSILLE:　Anyway, I thank you; I can't say it enough.

HENRI:　I know you're not ungrateful. You'll return the favour some day—maybe sooner than you think.

BOUSILLE:　I don't see how. I never seem to have a single old penny to knot in the corner of a handkerchief.

HENRI:　Who's talking about money? Don't bother me with such material concerns! You seem to have nothing else on your mind!

PHIL:　Bousille, old pal, in this rotten world, it isn't every day that you'll meet a philanthropist like this.

HENRI, *indicating* PHIL:　He's a great one to talk about the good deeds of others, but he doesn't say a word about the sacrifices *he* made for you.

PHIL:　Bah! You're embarrassing me.

HENRI, *to* BOUSILLE:　Let me refresh your memory: you come out of the hospital expecting to join the bread line. But no: just like magic, you find yourself back at your machine in the glove factory, thanks to this wizard, who put in a good word for you with the fore-lady.

PHIL, *confessing*:　It wasn't easy: she wouldn't agree to a thing, that night!

HENRI:　Fifteen days later—wham!—you're out on your ear again.

BOUSILLE:　It was all on account of my confounded knee-cap, which wouldn't heal properly. After working the pedals all day long at the machine, my knee would swell like a watermelon. It hurt so much I was all in a sweat.

HENRI:　All the same, there you were, flat on your back! An invalid, unable to earn your living!

BOUSILLE:　I was really down, that Friday night.

HENRI:　So Phil played the Good Samaritan again: "Come

to our house!" he tells you. You show up with your rags—bingo!—Aurore sets you up a nice cot in the attic over the garage. Quite a break for a beggar, eh?

BOUSILLE: I appreciate it, you can be sure.

PHIL: No kidding, you're as happy there as a squirrel in a sack of nuts!

HENRI: Besides, manna from heaven falls for you every Saturday night! How much do you give him, Phil?

PHIL, *emphatically*: A big fat five bucks! [*He takes a bill from his pocket.*] Which reminds me, I forgot to give you your fee for this week.

BOUSILLE: I can wait.

PHIL, *placing the bill in his hand*: Believe me: there's a special providence watching over you.

BOUSILLE: It's quite plain. Only while we're on the subject of my work—

PHIL: You're not complaining, I hope? A few odd jobs at the garage, from time to time, to keep you from evil thoughts.

BOUSILLE: Evil thoughts I could overcome by myself, you know.

PHIL: How I envy you!

BOUSILLE: You put me in full charge of the gas pump— Sundays as well as during the week—

PHIL: I trust you.

BOUSILLE: But if, sometimes, I give you the impression of falling behind a little, believe me, I'm not doing it on purpose.

PHIL: Of course not!

BOUSILLE: No, it's just that the pain in my knee comes back when I'm on my bad leg for too long. Yesterday, for instance, I walked around quite a bit, you know. Well, my knee ached all night.

PHIL: It feels better this morning?

BOUSILLE: It's still awfully sensitive. What's more, it's

drizzling today. Say a little prayer that I don't bang it.

PHIL: Of course, you never could stand pain too well.

BOUSILLE: I humbly admit it: back in the days when Christians were thrown to the lions, I would have made a pretty ridiculous martyr.

PHIL: Me too! I would have set a mighty poor example for the next one.

HENRI, *coming closer*: You know, Phil, I just had an idea: we might still be able to do something more for this cry-baby.

PHIL: I bet you've just had a stroke of ... kind genius.

HENRI: What would you say, Bousille old man, to the job of doorman at the College?

BOUSILLE, *struck*: What?

HENRI: A beautiful clean room all to yourself, close to the chapel for your devotions! Sitting like a cabinet minister in front of a telephone and a loudspeaker! Your only work: calling the students to the parlour on holidays!

BOUSILLE, *dazzled*: That would be heaven!

HENRI: A thousand bucks a year! That's not chicken feed!

BOUSILLE: Then I could pay you back.

PHIL: Better still. A thousand bucks! Think of it. With a four-figure income like that you could afford a motor-scooter, kiddo! A scooter, imagine! Any colour you like.

HENRI: No more dragging your feet! No more lousy pain in your knee to wrinkle your forehead and break our hearts!

BOUSILLE: It sure is the walking that kills me.

HENRI: Old man Lafrance is getting so blind he's bumping his clay pipe against every wall.

BOUSILLE, *with honest concern*: But I wouldn't want him to be fired on account of me.

HENRI: Oh, no! His goose is cooked, anyway. It's only a matter of days before he lands on the dump. I'm surprised you didn't know: it's all over town. No need to tell you, the candidates are already lining up: a chance like that comes just once in a lifetime!

BOUSILLE: You could get me the position, you think?

HENRI: Under normal circumstances and with my political influence I could guarantee it with a clear conscience! But suppose for a moment that Bruno is convicted: can you see me standing before the Brother Director, with my head hanging? Me, Henri Gravel, the brother of a guy who'd been convicted of killing one of his fellow-men with his fists? I could never swing it for you, then. [*Under* BOUSILLE's *nose.*] No. Let's face the facts: if I'm to succeed in arranging the deal for you, Bruno has to be acquitted—no more, no less.

PHIL: Arrested in error, released with honour!

HENRI: The accused? Just a fine boy from St. Tite, who had the guts to stand up to a pipsqueak from Montreal who tried to seduce his girl. Then it's another story, believe me: everyone in the village crows about it! And I bring you your contract, signed, sealed and delivered, with the key to the College on a silver platter!

BOUSILLE: It sounds too good to be true!

HENRI, *significantly*: It all depends on you, old man.

BOUSILLE: How's that?

HENRI, *changing his tone, and bringing his chair closer to* BOUSILLE's: Have you thought over what I told you last night?

BOUSILLE: Last night?

HENRI: Before you left for St. Tite?

BOUSILLE, *beginning to understand*: Oh! Yes.

HENRI: You see, there's a little point in the story you gave the lawyer that's not quite precise. Just a shade, mind you, but it could be taken by the jury in one of two ways—and make all the difference in the world to the verdict. So, if you agree, we'll try and throw a little light on the subject.

71

BOUSILLE: Personally, I'm all in favour of getting everything cleared up.

HENRI: It concerns your version of the fight between Bruno and Marc. The beginning makes good sense, but the end is mixed up like hell. . . . A second blow—given—not given—with a mumbo-jumbo remark by Bruno. [*Exaggerating purposely.*] You seem to be under the impression that—perhaps—you heard him mutter some kind of a . . . vague threat about a letter—

BOUSILLE, *interrupting*: Excuse me a second: I am not under an *impression*: I am *sure,* unfortunately.

HENRI: Now, look!

BOUSILLE: He said it clearly. I'm sorry.

HENRI: Yeah! Only you'd better listen to me, instead of babbling nonsense about something you heard in a dream. Understand? [*He drops his hand heavily on* BOUSILLE'S *knee.*]

BOUSILLE, *moaning and pulling his knee away*: Be careful!

HENRI: Oh! Is it *that* sensitive?

BOUSILLE: I can't say it enough.

HENRI, *after a pause*: Feel better now?

BOUSILLE: Yes, the pain is easing . . . slowly.

HENRI: Take care of it, eh? An ounce of prevention, you know.

BOUSILLE: Sure.

HENRI: Take good care, Especially since—and I repeat—when someone crosses me, I lose all control. Anything can happen. It's my pet weakness. You follow me?

BOUSILLE: Of course: it's not your fault.

HENRI: You wouldn't want to have a rock bounced off it?

BOUSILLE: No.

HENRI: Then let's try to agree. For instance, getting back to your story, I tell you right off, I'm not buying it.

BOUSILLE: To help you understand, I'll explain once

again exactly what took place, even if it upsets me to talk about it.

HENRI: You'd be wasting your breath: my mind's made up.

BOUSILLE: But—how can you know? At that time you were up in the clouds, flying away on your honeymoon.

HENRI: Listen to me: after the first blow, Marc stayed down for the count. The match was over—finished!

BOUSILLE: That's funny: only five minutes ago you were saying I had a memory like an elephant. Now everything I remember is all wrong.

PHIL, *cutting in*: Trust *him,* not your imagination. You won't regret it!

BOUSILLE: Yes, but—

HENRI: You see, the trouble with you is that your head is swollen, as well as your knee.

BOUSILLE: That's very possible.

HENRI: You're the only witness; you have no proof to support your claim: you could make up the wildest cock-and-bull story and everybody would have to take your word for it.

BOUSILLE: I mean—

HENRI: According to you, there are only two infallible people on earth: the Pope in Rome and Bousille in Montreal. "That's the truth no discussion period!"

BOUSILLE: What you just said there is a bit insulting to the Holy Father, you know.

HENRI: Yes, but you must admit that in your particular case, when *you* make a statement, we're entitled to a little doubt.

BOUSILLE: A big doubt.

HENRI: Well then, the lawyer himself said in this very room last night: "Any doubt must favour the accused." In other words, if there is the least doubt, Bruno must be given a chance: the law says so in big type.

BOUSILLE: If there is a doubt, as you claim, stop worrying: the judge will see it right away and declare Bruno not guilty.

HENRI, *swallowing his rage*: I want *you* to settle the question, instead of the judge, understand? I don't trust him, as I told you before.

BOUSILLE, *astounded*: But . . . I'm not qualified to do his work!

HENRI *hits* BOUSILLE'S *knee again; the latter doubles over in pain.*

HENRI: Will you stop bucking? You stupid mule! [*He goes to the dresser and fills his glass again.*]

PHIL, *less and less in agreement with* HENRI: Listen, Bousille: I admit Henri has all the fine instincts of a bouncer. But on your part you must confess that you're a bit slow on the uptake. After all, what he's asking you is simple enough.

BOUSILLE, *his head bowed*: I know I'm not intelligent. Why can't you accept it? At school it never failed: I was always the last to catch on at the back of the class. Luckily, the teacher was patient. She knew that I tried my very best and that my father would give me another beating if I failed my grade again. So, instead of pushing me around, like you now, she kept me after school. We'd say a little prayer to the Holy Ghost. Then we'd pull together, trying to make me understand. And sometimes it worked.

PHIL, *feeling more compassion than he cares to show*: Listen, Bousille: it's not a question of pushing you around, but—

HENRI, *already confronting* BOUSILLE, *his eyes hard*: So, you want a private lesson, eh? Okay, you little pinhead! Get your slate out; I'll dictate your homework for today. Take it down word for word, if you don't want to see your father's ghost! [*Grabbing him by the lapel of his coat.*] When the lawyer asks you if anything happened after Marc fell, you say, "No." [*He goes on, despite* BOUSILLE's *stupefaction.*] I'm not asking you to invent a detective story and get yourself balled up. All you have to say on the subject is "No"—N, O, No! Is that clear?

BOUSILLE, *flabbergasted*: But I can't say "No" when—

HENRI, *slapping him across the face*: Do you want me to carve it on your forehead?

PHIL: Just a minute, Henri! [*He comes between them and tries to calm* HENRI *down.*] Let me talk to the guy. I'm used to him.

HENRI, *drawing off, consulting his watch*:   Make it snappy: it's twenty to ten. What's more, I'm getting fed up to the teeth!

PHIL, *to* BOUSILLE: You heard that? I'm afraid you've got too much faith in your lucky star, my daring little friend. I'm telling you, it's getting stormy mighty fast. If the thunder crashes over your head, you run the risk of being badly messed up. Don't you think so?

BOUSILLE: No. They say only the lightning is dangerous.

PHIL, *deflated*:   Of course! When the bang comes, it's already too late: the damage is done! You've understood that once and for all. That's your strength, when the going gets tough. You know you're too shortsighted to see the danger coming, anyway: so why worry and get all upset?

BOUSILLE: That's exactly what Father Sébastien so often tells me: "Why worry and torment yourself? You're in the hands of God." Besides, our Saviour said: "Not a hair of your head will perish without the permission of my Father who is in heaven."

PHIL: Holy cow! Maybe you don't hold the floor at parties, but when you're quizzed on your speciality you sure handle yourself like the Boy Jesus in the Temple!

HENRI, *who has been restraining his wrath, comes towards them*:   All right! That's enough of the Bible!

PHIL: Keep your shirt on, will you? Can't you see we're not through with our little summit conference?

HENRI: I give you thirty seconds, not a tick more.

PHIL: The moment will come soon enough to give the signal for slaughter. Eh, Bousille? [BOUSILLE *agrees, rather lost.*] First, let me ask you a little personal question: are you frank enough to admit you've told a lie, sometimes?

BOUSILLE, *searching his conscience for a moment*:   It could happen to me, like anybody else.

PHIL: Sure, you're a member of our union, too. Well, my fine-feathered friend, all Henri's asking you is to play a good trick on the judge and slip one past him. Just a tiny two-letter fib, in one second flat!

BOUSILLE, *murmering, astonished*:   What?

PHIL: Nobody can contradict you: you're the only witness. It's a perfect set-up, I tell you.

BOUSILLE: I'm sorry, but I'm afraid I understand even less than ever.

PHIL: How's that? Did I leave out some piddling little detail by mistake?

BOUSILLE: Before I tell this little fib, as you call it, I'm sure you forgot the book I'll place my hand on.

PHIL, *taking* BOUSILLE's *prayer-book*:   On one like this, poor fellow! [*He opens it at random and reads:*] "At that time, Jesus said to his disciples: Verily, verily, I say unto you . . ." [*Closing it again.*] You see: there's everything you need in there. Don't tell me your own prayer-book scares you that much! You carry it under your arm every morning on the way to six- o'clock mass.

BOUSILLE: And you want me to do what Henri is asking— after I swear on *that* to tell the truth, and nothing but the truth?

PHIL: That's all! You see, you didn't need to buck so long.

HENRI, *jolly*: Did you think the clerk was going to make you drop an atom bomb?

PHIL: I knew we'd finally succeed in explaining the problem to him in all its brilliant simplicity!

HENRI: My dear fellow-citizen, give me your whole-hearted support, as the politician says, and the damn thing breezes by the judge's nose like the noon express past the station!

PHIL: Bruno falls into his mother's arms: she opens the flood-gates, and soaks his tie. Everybody in the house dances for joy! The children sing, "Alleluia!" The dog barks. The goldfish go crazy! And *you*, in your corner, you survey the scene with the satisfaction of a duty well done, saying to yourself: "*I* know the anonymous bene-factor who brought happiness to this lovely big family."

HENRI: But don't look for me in the picture: I'm already at the College, fixing you up with that job. Before the end of the month the Brothers must be waiting for you on the front steps, smiling from ear to ear!

PHIL: Watch out! Here you come on your scooter, back-firing like a show-off from the city! Here . . . [*Producing his money-roll.*] I'm so anxious to see you flashing around on that gem that I'm giving you a present of fifty dollars, right now, for your first instalment.

HENRI, *producing his own roll*: I'll raise you: one hundred bucks!

PHIL: Did you hear that? One hundred and fifty smackers! Oscar Perron will give you credit for the rest: you can have it right in front of the house tomorrow night.

HENRI, *thrusting the bills under* BOUSILLE's *nose*: What do you say to that, my boy?

BOUSILLE, *at last understanding fully* HENRI's *intentions*: You *can't* ask me to do such a thing.

HENRI: What?

BOUSILLE: You know very well I'd be committing per-jury.

77

HENRI: Listen, you—

BOUSILLE, *terrified*: Then God would let me drop like a stone into drunkenness again; I'm dead sure of it!

HENRI, *in a cold rage*: I'm giving you fair warning: the time for jokes is over.

BOUSILLE, *lost in his obsession*: I had a poor uncle who suffered a terrible punishment for committing a crime like this, you know it—

PHIL, *realizing the issue will go further than he had foreseen*: My advice is to forget it, Henri.

BOUSILLE, *his breath failing, fumbles in his pocket for his pills*: If you'd seen him there—as I will, forever: he ran and ran like a man possessed! Blood flowed all over!

PHIL, *to* HENRI: You'll never break him down!

HENRI: We'll see about that.

BOUSILLE: He cried: "God has punished me! God has punished me!"

HENRI, *shouting*: Enough!

BOUSILLE, *about to swallow a pill, stops, stunned. Silently,* HENRI *moves towards him and knocks the bottle away, scattering its contents across the room. Then, with a violent blow on the shoulder, he sends* BOUSILLE *reeling onto the luggage rack.* BOUSILLE, *up to the end of the scene, makes no effort to defend himself.*

PHIL, *sickened*: No, Henri, no! It's not worth the risk!

HENRI, *to* PHIL, *indicating the prayer-book*: Shut up, you. Hand me that.

PHIL, *giving it to him, unable to resist*: I've always given in to you. I'm yellow, and you know it. But now, I'm telling you, if you've got the least bit of heart—

HENRI, *crushing him*: I said, "Shut up!" [*Hard as steel, confronting* BOUSILLE.] You'll swear to testify as I told you.

BOUSILLE, *looking at him, appalled*: You don't understand.

HENRI, *holding out the prayer-book to him*: You'll swear on that!

BOUSILLE: No.

HENRI, *slapping him*: You hear?

BOUSILLE: You'll destroy me!

HENRI: Swear!

BOUSILLE: You'll destroy me! I can't say—

HENRI: God damn you! [*With all his weight, he applies his knee to the outstretched leg of* BOUSILLE, *whose unfinished sentence ends in a moan: he faints, his head falling against* HENRI's *stomach.*]

HENRI, *to* PHIL: Get me that glass. [*He indicates his half-full glass of alcohol.*]

PHIL, *green with fear, bringing the glass*: Be careful, Henri: you know he's got a weak heart!

HENRI: Go to hell! [*To* BOUSILLE, *who comes to and moans feebly.*] Snap out of it. I'm wise to your phony fits.

BOUSILLE, *murmuring, still half-conscious*: You don't understand.

HENRI, *forcing the glass to* BOUSILLE's *lips*: Drink this.

BOUSILLE: You'll destroy me! I can't say it enough!

HENRI: Come on, down it. [*He makes him swallow a mouthful, which* BOUSILLE *half spits out as he recognizes the taste of alcohol.* HENRI *retrieves the prayer-book.*] Swear. [*Refusing,* BOUSILLE *shakes his head.*] Do you want another dose?

BOUSILLE: No!

PHIL, *terrified also*: Give in, Bousille, for your own sake.

BOUSILLE, *in a fog*:   I don't know any more—

HENRI: *I* know. [*Holding* BOUSILLE's *hand on the prayer-book.*] You swear to do what I told you? [*Not satisfied with* BOUSILLE's *vague nod.*] Say "Yes," you bastard—

PHIL: Say "Yes," Bousille, quick!

HENRI, *his knee over* BOUSILLE's: Or I'll break this in two!

PHIL: He'll do it, Bousille!

BOUSILLE, *whispering*: Yes.

PHIL: Let him go, Henri! Let him go! He swore!

HENRI, *dropping* BOUSILLE'S *hand and removing his knee*: You realize what you just did? You've no more choice now. [*Consulting his watch.*] Get up: it's time to go.

PHIL, *helping* BOUSILLE *to his feet*: Come on, Bousille.

BOUSILLE, *completely dazed*: God is my witness: I didn't want to do it.

PHIL, *helping him back into his raincoat*: You had no way out, Bousille, believe me.

HENRI: For the first time in your life you've acted like a man. [*He pushes him towards the door.*] Move!

BOUSILLE: God is my witness—

HENRI, *opening the door*: Get going!

PHIL: Come along, Bousille, old pal. [*He leads* BOUSILLE *to the exit.*]

Curtain.

ACT TWO

SCENE TWO

As the curtain rises, the MOTHER *is lying in bed, a damp towel on her brow. Near her, a glass of water, medicine, her beads, and sundry other items clutter up the night-stand. Sitting on the luggage rack at the foot of the bed, Brother* THÉOPHILE *is reading to her.*

THÉOPHILE, *reading*: "As Reverend Father Vincent wrote in his study on Grace, considered not so much as a gratuitous gift of God but even more as a retribution— or better still, as a recompense that one must ceaselessly merit anew, at the price of daily mortification, constantly renewed and accepted, in the renunciation of self, of one's personal preferences, and of those thousand little things, which are the essence of—"

MOTHER, *her head splitting*: Théophile!

THÉOPHILE: Yes, Auntie?

MOTHER: Théophile, you're a good boy, but stop reading: you're getting on my nerves!

THÉOPHILE, *not losing countenance*: Very well, Auntie.

MOTHER, *handing* NOELLA *the wet towel*: Noella, will you get me a fresh one?

NOELLA: Why don't you try to doze off a few minutes?

MOTHER, *moaning*: I can't. Black thoughts keep tumbling around in my head, like dirty clothes in a washing machine.

THÉOPHILE, *stifling a yawn*: Indeed, Auntie, it seems to me a bit of sleep would benefit you greatly. Besides, I'll have to leave soon, much to my regret.

MOTHER: Don't stay on my account.

THÉOPHILE, *consulting a large silver pocket watch*: Twenty-five after four already! The Brother Cook is coming to collect a load of potatoes at Bonsecours Market at four-thirty, and he has graciously offered to pick me up downstairs in the Order's truck.

MOTHER: Better get ready, so you won't keep him waiting.

THÉOPHILE: I was just going to say so; at this time of day it would be difficult for him to park in front of the hotel. NOELLA *comes silently and places another towel on the* MOTHER's *forehead.*

MOTHER: Thank you, Noella, dear. But what in the world is keeping the children from 'phoning any news?

THÉOPHILE: I'm certain they'll call as soon as they have some.

MOTHER: Surely that stupid trial should be over by now. Phil said at noon that all the witnesses had been heard.

THÉOPHILE: Am I to understand that Bousille finally testified today?

MOTHER, *dolefully*: This morning, yes. That sweet child Colette, too.

THÉOPHILE: I dare hope he acquitted himself with honour.

MOTHER: Ask Noella: nobody tells me anything any more.

NOELLA, *laconically bringing* THÉOPHILE *his hat and coat*: It went as Henri wished.

THÉOPHILE: God be praised! Only yesterday morning, Bousille confided to me that the fear of making a mistake was constantly on his mind. I'm sorry I must leave without saying goodbye to him.

NOELLA: You couldn't have seen him, anyway; Phil made him take the bus to St. Tite right after the hearing at noon.

THÉOPHILE: Oh, really? He's gone?

NOELLA: Yes, he was completely exhausted.

THÉOPHILE: Please thank Cousin Vézina on my behalf for his touching solicitude. Later I'll go to the chapel and offer a little prayer for him.

NOELLA: Pray most of all for your poor Bousille. [*Not wanting to say more.*] He must be very unhappy at this moment.

THÉOPHILE: I'm afraid so. The outcome of the trial worries him greatly.

MOTHER: Why don't they 'phone, those idiots?

THÉOPHILE, *near the bed, hat and book in hand*: Well, then, goodbye, Auntie. And be of good faith. I'll return to comfort you tomorrow afternoon, if you're still in the same condition.

MOTHER, *panic-stricken at the thought*: You poor boy! If the trial drags on till then, I warn you, you'll find me in my coffin.

THÉOPHILE, *who has a one-track mind*: Until then, take courage by thinking of our Lady of the Seven Sorrows, during the Passion of her beloved Son.

MOTHER: Poor Blessed Virgin! If she suffered as much as I do now, how I pity her!

THÉOPHILE: As for me, I'll keep praying that justice be done.

MOTHER: Pray that we win: that's all I ask!

THÉOPHILE: Very well, Auntie.

MOTHER: Good St. Ann, if you're the least bit on my side, please make them 'phone!

THÉOPHILE, *taking leave of* NOELLA: Have faith, too, Mrs. Gravel.

NOELLA: Goodbye, Théophile. Thank you for coming.

The ring of the telephone fills the room. Everybody jumps. The MOTHER, *as if projected by a spring, throws away the towel she had on her forehead and gets up on her knees in bed.*

MOTHER, *spluttering, while* NOELLA *goes to the telephone*: Dear Lord! Good St. Ann, take pity on your daughter!

NOELLA, *on the telephone, tense in spite of herself*: Hello? ... Pardon me?

MOTHER: What does he say? Quick: it's killing me!

NOELLA, *to* THÉOPHILE, *who is also in suspense, his neck outstretched towards the telephone*: It's Brother Stanislas, waiting for you in the lobby.

The MOTHER *falls back on the bed with a long moan.*

NOELLA, *on the telephone*: He'll be right down! [*She hangs up, and cannot refrain from rubbing her forehead.*]

THÉOPHILE, *clearing his throat to hide his embarrassment*: I'm sorry, Auntie. I'm sure you would have preferred some news—especially good news.

MOTHER, *pitiably*: Good St. Ann, I'm getting tired of always repeating the same thing to you!

THÉOPHILE: Arm yourself with patience, Auntie: you know, some trials last two or three weeks.

MOTHER, *moaning*: Don't say that: I'll skin you alive!

THÉOPHILE, *retreating*: Very well, then. .... And once again, be of good faith.

PHIL *storms in.*

PHIL, *shouting, arms outstretched*: Glory, alleluiah!

MOTHER, *now petrified, eyes popping*: Eh? ... What?

PHIL, *coming to the bed and shaking her by the shoulders*: I said, "Alleluiah!" my dear mother-in-law. Well, go on, have your heart attack!

MOTHER, *fearing the shock of understanding*: You don't mean that ...?

PHIL: Sure enough! Your little choir boy has just been acquitted by a mile!

MOTHER, *coming out of the fog, slowly but surely*: No! Not really?

PHIL: Sounds like fairy a tale, but it's the honest truth! [*It is obvious that he has not waited for the verdict to begin his thanksgiving binge.*]

MOTHER: I can't believe it.

PHIL: Come on, force yourself! The case is dismissed with a swift kick in the procedure.

MOTHER, *crying*: Oh, I'm so happy! ... I'm so happy!

NOELLA, *approaching him*: The verdict has just been given?

PHIL: Right this minute! The judge hasn't even had time to leave with his golf clubs yet!

MOTHER, *completely restored*: Where is he? I want to see him right away and hold him in my arms. The poor boy suffered so much for nothing.

PHIL: They'll release him any moment. Just give them time to screw his halo back on his head and slip his flask into his hand.

MOTHER: Oh, dear! I'll never be ready! [*All excited.*] Noella, quick! Come and help me. [*Without even putting on her shoes, she runs to the other room, followed by* NOELLA.] I'm so anxious! [*Disappearing.*] So anxious to see him!

THÉOPHILE, *who has been waiting, comes forward, beaming*: May I congratulate you, Cousin Vézina?

PHIL, *seeing him for the first time, shudders*: Oh, no! Just the guy I wanted to dodge today!

THÉOPHILE: First of all, let me tell you how much I admired your courage, all of you, during this terrible ordeal.

PHIL: Courage? I'd say we had the nerve of a skunk.

THÉOPHILE: All that proves a great truth—

PHIL: I bet you're coming out with another lulu!

THÉOPHILE: Those who place all their trust in divine Justice are never disappointed.

PHIL: How true! How very true! Write that one down on a piece of paper. It's too good; I must tell it to the guys back in St. Tite.

THÉOPHILE, *holding forth with the full strength of his candour*: Before departing, I'd like to take this opportunity to thank you and the entire family for your understanding and generosity towards my poor Bousille.

PHIL: You're killing me! Have you any more like that?

THÉOPHILE: He's so defenceless, it would have been easy for unscrupulous people to take advantage of his innocence.

PHIL: Don't kid yourself: he gave us one hell of a time!

THÉOPHILE: I know all the sacrifices you have made for him, including your thoughtful gesture today.

PHIL, *taking him by the shoulders*: You'll never believe me in all your sinful life, but that gesture is exactly what I've been trying so hard to forget ever since.

THÉOPHILE: But be sure of one thing: the more you try to forget it, the more God will remember it.

PHIL: Will you stop scaring me?

THÉOPHILE: And you may be sure He'll pay you back a hundredfold.

PHIL: You can be cruel as hell!

THÉOPHILE: I simply repeat His own words: "As long as you did it to one of these my least brethren, you did it to Me."

PHIL: That's it: kick as hard as you can! Don't miss the chance: you've got me with my pants down!

THÉOPHILE, *slightly at a loss*: Well, then, I'll say goodbye. ... And once again, be of good faith—er, I mean, congratulations!

PHIL, *shaking his hand*: Same to you, old man! See you on Judgment Day!

Retreating with as much dignity as possible, THÉOPHILE *collides with* AURORE, *who comes in like a whirlwind.*

AURORE, *ignoring* THÉOPHILE, *who picks up his hat and leaves*: Mother! Where are you?

MOTHER, *falling into her arms*: Aurore! Aurore!

AURORE: You heard the news?

MOTHER, *without waiting for the end of the question*: Ah! I can't believe it.

AURORE: I've never been so excited in all my life! [*She disappears into the bathroom.*]

MOTHER: It's a real miracle! [*She returns quickly to the other room.*]

PHIL, *pouring himself a drink*: No doubt about it. Too bad I already believe. A miracle like this would make me see the light in a flash!

MOTHER, *reappearing briefly in the doorway*: I told you so last night: he's no more rotten than the rest of the family.

PHIL: No, ma'am; no use looking for anyone more rotten than we are: you'd be wasting your time. [*Realizing he is alone in the room.*] Wouldn't you know it? For once in my life I had the guts to tell the truth, and not a living soul around to hear me!

AURORE, *coming out of the bathroom*: Let's hurry: Henri is down in the car. He wants us all to go and wait for Bruno in front of the Court House.

MOTHER, *shouting from the next room*: Won't be long!

AURORE, *to* PHIL: Call the bellboy to take down the luggage.

PHIL, *charitably pouring himself another drink*: Hold your horses! This camel needs a little more juice before crossing the desert.

AURORE, *retouching her lips in front of the mirror*: I know some gossips in St. Tite who'd better shut their traps if they don't want us to throw a libel suit at their heads.

MOTHER, *darting in for her bag*: Blessed St. Ann will have her pilgrimage, I'm warning you! [*She darts back into the next room.*]

PHIL, *muttering to himself*: I'll supply the beer! [*On the telephone, glass in hand.*] Hello! This is 312. Just letting you know the whole mob is shoving off. Send up the boy to bring down the ammunition, will you? . . . That's it, yes! It's years since we've been on a picnic, so now we're going on a pilgrimage! [*He hangs up.*]

MOTHER, *coming in, coat and hat on, handbag on her arm*: Let's go: I'm all ready.

PHIL: It's none of my damn' business, dear lady, but if you walk about on the street like that you'll get bunions.

MOTHER, *noticing she is still in her stocking feet*: Look at that! Can I be losing my mind? [*She hurries to put her shoes on*].

PHIL, *between his teeth*: Another useless question!

AURORE, *packing, with* NOELLA'S *help*: I hope I'll have a minute to get a doll for Gisèle: I promised her a present.

PHIL, *still muttering to himself*: And I'll try to find a nice little black-jack for Gaston: that child should be learning how to get along in the world!

AURORE: I've got to buy something for Mrs. Larose, too: she's taken care of the house for the last two days.

PHIL, *picking up Bruno's photograph*: Don't forget the picture of Al Capone!

MOTHER: Bless his sweet little heart! [*She kisses the photograph before slipping it into her bag.*]

AURORE, *taking the statue of St. Ann from the dresser*: Here's your miraculous statue.

MOTHER, *dramatically, statue in hand*: Silence a minute! Before we leave, let's all get down on our knees, together as never before, and give thanks to St. Ann for all she's done for us.

AURORE, *as the* MOTHER *kneels down*: Now, Mamma, don't you start in on your litanies again!

PHIL: Why wear out your praying machine? We got what we wanted.

MOTHER: Yes, but—

The telephone rings.

AURORE: Come on! You can say your little devotions some other time. [*She goes to the telephone.*]

PHIL: Sure. Everything's fine now: let's save our prayers for the next time we're in a mess!

AURORE, *already on the telephone*: What? ... [*To the others.*] St. Tite calling.

PHIL, *surprised*: St. Tite?

AURORE, *on the telephone*: Hello! ... Yes, Mrs. Larose?

HENRI, *bursting into the room*: What's keeping you, for God's sake? Hurry up, damn it!

MOTHER, *picking up her bag*: I'm going down right now!

[*She rushes out.*]

PHIL, *approaching* AURORE, *anxiously*: What is it?

AURORE, *dazed, letting the receiver fall*: Gisèle ...

PHIL, *suddenly sobered*: What's the matter?

AURORE, *in a dead voice*: ... found Bousille ... in the attic over the garage ... hanged!

NOELLA *hides her face in her hands. The others remain stunned.*

AURORE: The police want us back for the inquest.

After a leaden silence, HENRI *lowers his head, staring vacantly.*

PHIL, *through his teeth, turning slowly towards* HENRI: You

wanted to avoid a scandal: now try and get us out of
this one—you son-of-a-bitch!

Nobody moves, while NOELLA *recites under her breath
what might be the* De Profundis. *The curtain falls.*